Shakespeare and the Young Writer

Fred Sedgwick's new book presents case studies of children in primary schools writing in the grip of studying Shakespeare. It follows his earlier book for Routledge *Read my Mind* which has a similar focus on creativity, but here Shakespeare is the basis for inspiration.

Teachers will find the book useful in teaching literacy, whether within the confines of current educational policy or in the richer context of understanding the language of poetry and drama. There is ample evidence of children responding to Shakespeare's ideas and furthering their own perceptions as a result.

Filled with extraordinary children's writing and practical guidance for teachers, this is a necessary tool for all teachers anxious to improve their practice: to teach literacy well but also to teach humanity.

Fred Sedgwick has many years of experience as a freelance teacher, lecturer and writer. He is the author of *Read my Mind* (1997) and *Thinking about Literacy* (1999) for Routledge and is actively involved in all aspects of children's learning.

D0072091

Shakespeare and the Young Writer

Fred Sedgwick

London and New York

First published 1999
by Routledge
11 New Fetter Lane, London EC4P 4EE

Simultaneously published in the USA and Canada
by Routledge
29 West 35th Street, New York, NY 10001

Routledge is an imprint of the Taylor & Francis Group

Typeset in Goudy by Routledge
Printed and bound in Great Britain by
Biddles Ltd, Guildford and King's Lynn

British Library Cataloguing in Publication Data
A catalogue record for this book is available from the British
Library

Library of Congress Cataloging in Publication Data
Sedgwick, Fred.
Shakespeare and the young writer / Fred Sedgwick.
p. cm.
Includes bibliographical references and index.
1. Shakespeare, William, 1564–1616–Study and teaching (Primary)–
Great Britain. 2. Drama in education. I. Title.
PR2987.S39   1999   98–50231
822.3`3–dc21   CIP

ISBN 0–415–17468–6 (hbk)
ISBN 0–415–17469–4 (pbk)

You go not till I set you up a glass
Where you may see the inmost part of you ...

(*Hamlet* III:4:19–20)

Contents

Acknowledgements   ix
Dedicatory poem   xi
A glass where you may see   xiii

Introduction   1

1 Mouth full of news: single lines and single speeches   20

2 Now it is the time of night: *A Midsummer Night's Dream*   39

3 A local habitation: *The Tempest* and *As You Like It*   65

  Interval: Thou drone, thou snail, thou slug, thou sot   77

4 How goes the night, boy? *Macbeth*   89

5 Bright smoke: *Romeo and Juliet*   108

6 Furious winter's rages: *King Lear* and *Cymbeline*   114

7 By heart   124

8 Faith, hope, love and teaching   136

  Afterword: the wind and the rain   141

Appendix   143
References   151
Index   157

Acknowledgements

Thank you to the teachers and children in primary schools where I have been allowed – even, occasionally, encouraged – to teach Shakespeare:

Fairlands Primary, St Nicholas Primary and Peartree Spring Juniors – all Stevenage; Purwell Primary, Hitchin; Ashwell Primary; Parkgate Infant and Parkgate Junior, Watford; Radburn Primary, Letchworth – all Hertfordshire

Bentley, Little Bealings, Tattingstone, Rose Hill, St Helen's, Clifford Road Primaries – all Ipswich, Suffolk

St George's Primary, Colchester; Earls Colne Primary; Howe Green House near Bishops Stortford (and Dot Patten especially); Bournes Green Junior, Southend; Ryedene Primary, Basildon – all Essex

Old Catton Middle, Tacolneston Primary, Thorpe St Andrew High and St Williams – all Norwich

Latymer All Saints C of E Primary, Enfield

Milton Road Junior, Cambridge

Ryvers and Foxborough Combined, both Langley; The Hawthorns Primary, Wokingham – all Berkshire

I also worked at Pearse House, Bishop's Stortford on their *Lending Our Minds Out* courses, where children spend between one and two days working with writers. Some of the work here comes from them.

Anyone writing about teaching Shakespeare is indebted to Rex Gibson, formerly at the University of Cambridge School of Education. His work on the 'Shakespeare in Schools Project' is invaluable, as are the newsletters of that project (now shamefully elusive) and his editions of Shakespeare's plays and poems (The Cambridge School Shakespeare).

Thank you to Gina Reid, for the vegetarian witches. Thank you to Delphine Ruston and Mary Moore for their helpful comments about teaching Shakespeare to secondary pupils, and to Diane Duncan, Mary Jane Drummond and Dennis Ruston for recollections of their own schooling. Thank you especially to Delphine Ruston again, and John Cotton, who read early drafts of this book and made many suggestions. Thanks, again, to Henry Burns Eliot and Emily Roeves. Thanks, most of all, to Dawn, who pointed out to me what I should have noticed – how child-like Bottom is and how Bottom-like children can be; and for helping to push this further: how much there is of children in Shakespeare and how much of Shakespeare's passion for humanity in all its forms there is in children.

I am grateful to the following publishers for permission to use short extracts from their editions of Shakespeare. These extracts are quoted by permission of Cambridge University Press, Oxford University Press and Thomas Nelson (The Arden Shakespeare). The extracts I have used from each edition are listed on pp. 149–50 and the editions used are listed on pp. 155–6.

Dedicatory poem
for John Cotton
friend, writer, teacher

Student actors 1966

He tucks twenty Players
    in his robes.
His eyelids flicker,
    tenser than shells,
as Make-up dabs swan's –
    egg green on them.

On stage Second Servant
    pops and plasters
blood in the grizzled beard.
    Cornwall puts
his foot down. Gloucester's
    thrust out to 'smell
His way to Dover'.
    They end each scene,
like the blinded duke,
    facing 'knowledge
of themselves'; and dying
    for a smoke.

(*King Lear* III:7:55–97; IV:5:272)

A glass where you may see

The voices of three children begin my book. They had read the two lines from *Hamlet* that I have used as an epigraph: 'You go not till I set you up a glass/Where you may see the inmost part of you' (*Hamlet* III:4:19–20). I asked them to write about 'what they would see if they held a mirror up to the secret places in their hearts and brains.…What animals or landscape would they see? What plants and vegetation? What colours and shapes? What textures? What feelings and emotions, what interests?' They wrote, guards lower than I'd expected, or they'd dreamt possible:

> You'd see my dark side…
> Blue and black with a flash of red for life.
> …You'd see my fears, life is my biggest fear.
> I'm small, the world's big…
>
> (Daniel, 11)

> …In my heart are various libraries for knowledge
> As I grow the libraries get bigger…
>
> (Jack, 11)

> …you would see a vast never-ending
> Desert where nothing lives. All is black like the moon.
> You could see the remains of a land once full of life,
> Skeletons of a land once full of life but only a small
> Fire glows. It is one light in a universe of darkness.
> But as the fire grows so does the black get darker and
> It seems futile to try to have a fire at all
> As something always comes with a blanket
> To suffocate my dream.
>
> (Chris, 11)

These are just extreme examples. Throughout this book, we can see evidence of children looking in mirrors, and understanding themselves better because of the extraordinary example of the 'tolerant humanism' of Shakespeare (Crick's phrase 1982, following Orwell). We can see their play with words leading to learning about themselves, their environments, their relationships and their language.

Introduction

For thirty-four years now – since my first teaching practice in Plymouth – I have been reading and reciting poetry to children. Mostly this has been for the sheer pleasure of it, and someday I would love to write a book about that pleasure: mine for certain, and the children's I hope. This pleasure is at least twofold: first, it is the music, sound and taste of the words, and second, it is in the understanding the words give us when we read them with care and attention. I read Charles Causley's *Figgie Hobbin* (1970 – but see 1996, where these poems are now collected) to a class in 1973, and a nine-year-old girl, Emma Bittleston, wrote to the poet: 'Sometimes I copy out your poems and pretend I am you'. I am sure that the poem 'Mary Mary Magdalene', from that book, helped her to anticipate love, marriage, child-bearing and widowhood, as much as 'I saw a jolly hunter' made her laugh. I wish her well now, wherever she is.

But sometimes I have read poems to children with a more specific purpose: to help them write their own poems. The aims of this writing was to enable them, through play with words, to learn about a curriculum I have already described like this: themselves, the world around them, the relationship between themselves and that world, and their language (Sedgwick 1997). I use the word 'play' advisedly for three reasons. First, I am convinced, like Caldwell Cook (1917), that

> when work and play are separated, the one becomes mere drudgery, the other mere pastime. Neither is then of any value in life. It is the core of my faith that only work worth doing is really play; for by play we mean the doing anything with one's heart in it...

Second, as Freud famously writes, 'The creative writer does the same as the child at play' (quoted in Vernon (ed.) 1970: 127). And finally, I suspect that the double meaning of the word 'play' – children's pleasurable imaginative activity, on the one hand, and drama on the other, is more than a coincidence.

Behind this practice has been the certainty that children writing poems without the experience of reading other poems – surprisingly, this is common –

means working in a field of ignorance. And, as Nabokov wrote: 'imagination without knowledge leads no further than the backyard of primitive art' (quoted in Meyer 1988). Mostly, for the purpose of getting children writing with some knowledge of what poetry can do, I have used the work of modern writers. For examples, see Sedgwick (1997), where children write under the influence of Craig Raine (p. 75), Edwin Morgan (pp. 83–4 and p. 127), John Cotton (p. 134), Adrian Henri (pp. 136–7), Miroslav Holub (pp. 73–4) and Gerda Meyer (p. 30). I have also used poems by Sylvia Plath (see especially her marvellous riddles for, respectively, an embryo (*Collected Poems*, p. 141) and a pregnancy (*Collected Poems*, p. 116).

One older example (the results of which, like the results of Plath's riddles, are not in my earlier book) is Thomas Hood's famous anthology piece, 'I remember, I remember' which my mother used to say to me, with a clip-clopping attention to metre and a midland Irish accent, when I was a boy ('I remember, I remember,/The house where I was born,/The little window where the sun/Came peeping in at morn…'). Under the influence of this poem, children have written these pieces:

> I remember, I remember
> When my parents divorced.
> I was four.
> I got up in the morning as usual.
> My Mum told me
> My Dad wasn't coming back.
> I remember, I remember
> The sharp pain
> That hit me all over,
> The sour smell
> That made me sick.
> I felt alone
> As if no-one could ever touch me again.
>
> (Jenny, 14)

Another child, who had spent months in hospital, wrote about 'coming home to a house I could not remember', and another wrote

> I remember
> when my mother took me to another house
> and I said
> why are we going here?
> and she said
> Don't you want Peter to be your new Dad?
> And I said Yes
> so he was.
>
> (Alison, 10)

So I knew from both intensive and extensive experience that children could write vividly and honestly using modern poets as yet unassessed by time, and also relatively minor writers like Hood whose place on Parnassus had been more or less settled. In the above examples, as with others I have collected, the writers seemed to be learning about their own feelings; here, pain and a resigned acceptance.

'Others', Matthew Arnold had written to Shakespeare in his sonnet, titled 'Shakespeare', 'abide our question. Thou art free'. I began to wonder what child-writers would achieve when they questioned, and were questioned by, Shakespeare. I'd always taken for granted that Shakespeare is simply 'too difficult' for primary children. I now know that I was mistaken. This book is a record of a project which ran alongside others (they were also concerned with children and their writing: see Sedgwick 1999 for one) which involved getting children aged between 6 and 14 composing in many settings – school halls, classrooms, on writing courses in Youth Hostels – with the example of abiding Shakespeare's freedom and humanity before them. Mostly they wrote poems. But they also wrote prose and, occasionally, dialogue.

A political perspective

I have to make one point concerned with the politics of the times. If a new humanistic hegemony arises, with people – children, teachers, parents – at its centre, rather than an abstract managerialism based on control, the comments that follow will soon be out of date. To expect that now, though, would be insanely optimistic. Children today (I am writing my final draft of this in September 1998) have to work at any subject for two dominating reasons: to succeed in tests and to help hoist their schools higher up the league tables. The strength of the hegemony that dictates this state of affairs is increased by the children's unawareness of it: they are innocent foot soldiers in a war in which the enemy has changed the strategic objectives of education from helping children in their learning and feeling to the achievement of satisfactory statistics.

Frequently, children are injured in that war. Here is one of the walking wounded, from an account by a secondary English teacher:

> ...last year I was supervising some low ability students who were allowed extra time for their SAT. Just after the test began one girl burst into tears. I took her outside the classroom and asked her what was the matter. She said she couldn't understand the question and was frightened by the whole thing – the exam paper, the silence, the long length of time she had to sit there. I asked her to tell me what the prescribed scene from *Romeo and Juliet* was all about: she knew it inside-out....When quizzed about character, dramatic qualities, theme, language, she knew all about that too. I reassured her that she could do the test and she went back in but it struck me how cruel it was to expose this weak, insecure girl to such

an unnecessary ordeal, especially when, before that moment, she had obviously loved the play...

(Ruston, private letter, 1998)

What are we to make of this? 'Low ability students'; a 'prescribed' scene; a child 'loves' a play but hates the test? It is an interesting trio: Child, Play, Test. For which should we have the most respect? A system in which test results have more impact on the politicians' assessment of a school than a child's understanding of a play is, literally, an inhuman one. It neglects the student's emotional life hinted at in this letter and, despite appearances, it neglects her understanding. Also, it is philistine because it attempts to reduce the play from the complex and exciting artefact that it is to a yardstick by which we can judge children. The child and the play rate way below the test. There is a fourth element I have not mentioned yet – the teacher. In modern Britain the teacher comes beneath, even, the child and the play. As Ruston goes on to say '...we don't have the choice to follow the students' or our own enthusiasm...'. Another teacher told me that she had 'four weeks to teach *Macbeth* to her Year-9s....I showed them the Polanski film in one session, maybe I'll concentrate on key scenes from now on.'

For me and for Ruston (and for countless other teachers of Shakespeare) children work for nobler motives than those imposed on that girl. D H Lawrence was aware of such motives when he taught *The Tempest*. He was also sensitive to the tension between those motives and his contemporary management:

A curious wailing of distressed voices issued from a far corner....The words of a familiar song arose from the depths: 'Full fathom five thy father lies;/Of his bones are coral made...' Lawrence rushed with outstretched hands to the visitor [an inspector]: 'Hush! Hush! Don't you hear? The sea chorus from *The Tempest*.'

(quoted in Worthen 1991: 208)

Lawrence may sound a little precious here (though who is to say that a less than respectful and more than ordinarily playful view of the inspector and all that the inspector stands for are not part of a slightly camp pose?). But his instinct is sound: 'Full fathom five' will always have more to say to teacher and child in a classroom than any inspector, than any politician, than any OFSTED report.

'Writing...is practically the only activity a person can do that is not competitive' wrote Paul Theroux in *Time* in 1978, and, more famously, William Blake said that 'Real Poets [cannot] have any competition. None are the greatest in the Kingdom of Heaven; it is so in Poetry' (1826). As competition is irrelevant to creative writing of all kinds, so tests are irrelevant to education; in particular, as far as I am concerned right now, right here, to education about Shakespeare's words. Young writers should be encouraged to use these words at school in their reading, writing, drama and art for the same broad purpose as they should be encouraged to use any other words: to help them to understand.

This is true of adults in the wider world as well, but in our puritanical and materialistic society the connection between enjoyment (what we hope for when we attend a play by Shakespeare) and learning (what inevitably happens in Shakespeare's theatre, however dull the production) is broken. Children though, 'trailing [their] clouds of glory', (as Wordsworth put it in his 'Ode: Intimations of Immortality from Recollections of Early Childhood') are still active learners, and do not, as a rule, screw their faces up at the thought of connecting entertainment with learning. Watch their eyes as they come into school expectantly at four years old, or nine o'clock every day, expecting to enjoy and to learn. If they learn to hate Shakespeare's work, or be bored by it, or be indifferent to it (as so many do) it is some adult's fault, or, more accurately, some system's; it is simply never theirs.

By responding to Shakespeare's poetry, children learn (the potential is there for ourselves as adults, too) about themselves: their loves, their horrors, their delights, their dreams, their eventual deaths. They learn about Shakespeare's language, and some of the reasons why it is held, almost universally, in such high esteem. They learn about language in general. And they learn about the relationship between themselves and all their experiences, and Shakespeare's language, and language in general. This learning is always active. It is by now a commonplace (except among politicians and their hired hands) that children are never passive receivers of information. In contrast, they are always constructing knowledge out of the interaction between themselves, that information and their teachers, or other adults working with them. Politicians of the entire political spectrum, then, who have conspired over the past twenty years to impose a mechanistic system on schools, with its resulting devaluation of the emotions and the arts, have devalued Shakespeare and education, and sold the children short. This is all part of what I call a cultural definition.

A cultural definition

I mean by 'cultural definition' how we, wittingly or unwittingly, define Shakespeare in our times as a society. In one school, three eleven-year-old girls gave me a scrap of paper when I arrived – they knew we were going to work on Shakespeare – that contributed to this definition. It read

Juliet—we shall meet tonight at twelve to be wed for evermore

Romeo, Romeo, wherefore art though Romeo

your eyes are as blue as the sky

your hair is brown as brown can be...

Vaguely recalled quotations usually misapplied and misunderstood, an equally vague romantic 'feeling', the clichés of love – these are all part of this cultural definition. But there is almost infinitely more – or so it feels. There has been, of course, much political – and even royal – discussion about Shakespeare and education. In 1989, Prince Charles attacked modern teaching of English and compared the way young people speak now with the glories of Shakespeare's English. Wheale identifies the politics of this kind of talk as an English 'nationalist agenda', and comments, rightly in my view,

> The Prince's summons leads us deep into the million strange shadows of ideology, in these forms: the language represented as an ideal cultural institution; an appeal to religious discourse and mystical categories; a version of national history as visionary national unity. And all of this bears down on the text called Shakespeare in ways in which it is deployed as a national scripture…equivalent to Common Prayer…
>
> (Aers and Wheale 1991: 6)

The Prince's words are shallow, and their unrecognized ideology is, in large part, in that shallowness. His Shakespeare is, in Styles' phrase (1998), 'a cliché of everything English'. He castigates modern use of 'casual obscenity' as though he had never read Malvolio's reading of Maria's letter in *Twelfth Night*, or the first scene of *Romeo and Juliet*, or Mercutio's speech at II:1:7–41. He should have read Eric Partridge's enlightening *Shakespeare's Bawdy* (1948) or chapter 5 of Hughes' *Swearing* (1998: 35) before he made such pronouncements.

The Prince's innocent version of Shakespeare is the one we are supposed to take for granted as the only one by those who make remarks like 'I do not think there is a place for the exposure of children to different critical approaches. That, if it has to be undertaken at all, should be undertaken in the universities' (Chris Woodhead quoted in Bottoms 1994: 25). As Janet Bottoms says, 'The implication that there is one obvious approach from which university students are lured into the trackless wastes of critical theory is, of course, nonsense'. It is also dangerous: suppose Woodhead had suggested that there was only one 'critical approach' to the history of the Russian or the French Revolution, or to the Second World War, or to the Slave Trade. We would see more clearly such thinking for what it is: verging on the totalitarian. And the Prince's approach, if resurrected in schools, would lead to an emasculated Shakespeare, serving the purposes of a minority, but powerful class.

At the other extreme, there are radical left critical approaches to Shakespeare. Bottoms (1994: 25) quotes Coles where 'she distinguished her own aim from that of those teachers who seek *merely* to foster…enjoyment' (Bottoms' italics). Bottoms (1994: 25) also quotes McEvoy, saying that the plays should be a 'site of conflict…where dominant readings are challenged and the ideological use of these texts is revealed by the production of oppositional readings'. I have been stirred, annoyed, provoked and depressed by many oppositional readings of Shakespeare's plays – see Hobby and Shepherd, for example in Aers and Wheale (1991). But I will make it implicitly clear throughout this book that I am pre-eminently concerned, alongside learning, with enjoyment. After all, these critics didn't become knowledgeable about Shakespeare without first enjoying him; and I feel, with Bottoms, that before children learn to 'read against the grain', they need to find out through their study in the classroom which way the grain runs.

Anyone concerned with children and books can only applaud the fact that 'the text we call Shakespeare' is debated so widely and so fiercely: it is a truism, after all, to say that Shakespeare's language is woven into almost all our speech and that he abides our question. 'If music be the food of love…Dying fall…take great exception…mistress mine…sweet and twenty…cakes and ale…some are born great, some achieve greatness, some have greatness thrust upon them…midsummer madness…the whole pack of you…hey, ho, the wind and the rain….' These phrases from just one play, *Twelfth Night*, demonstrate that we are often quoting Shakespeare when we don't know it. Of course, as Cotton has pointed out in a private letter (1998), we cannot be sure that these phrases are his own, and not phrases current at his time that he has incorporated into his plays: he was, after all, a gifted magpie, as we can see from his use of ancient plots from many different sources. This doesn't invalidate my point: the ubiquity of Shakespeare's words is a part of our cultural definition of him. We seem to understand implicitly that, if language is what makes us human, Shakespeare is an abiding light in the back of our minds that helps to keep us humane.

His work provides for us, as it has for our ancestors, benchmarks for our integrity. Emily Dickinson wrote 'I like a look of Agony/Because I know it's true'. All poets like that look too, and all humans know it is an honest look. Heaney will serve for an example when he writes about what's 'bitter' being what is also 'dependable' (1984: 15) and a character in A S Byatt's (1978: 108) novel 'saw the world *in extremis* and was right'. Shakespeare offers us hundreds of opportunities to see his characters facing up to the implacable realities of their natures and circumstances, and the relationship between those natures and those circumstances.

The character of Hamlet, for instance, exemplifies (among hundreds of other things) the human instinct for revenge moderated and frustrated by all kinds of moral anxieties. *Twelfth Night* and *Measure for Measure* hold mirrors up to our hardly-acknowledged sexual ambivalences, our moral laziness, our cruelty, our shallow puritanism, our self-deception, our vanity, our decadence. Macbeth makes us reflect on power and ambition, and how these things can, in the deepest sense, take away our humanity and send us to Hell: '…unsex me here,/And fill me from crown to toe top full/Of direst cruelty' prays Lady Macbeth as she resolves to become Queen by killing King Duncan. *Titus Andronicus*, with its sensationalist violence, relates to modern media violence, and teaches us that prurient interest in such violence is not new. Above all, *King Lear* demonstrates how all too often we have to become blind to see, have to become insane to understand. All this shows that Shakespeare is a critical part of our moral education – if in no other way, in the manner of his demonstrating the sheer complexity of decisions about right and wrong (in spite of dopey political rhetoric about the simplicity of such decisions).

Most of us accept, in an unreflective way, the cultural definition that insists that no English-speaking person is educated to any degree unless he or she has partial acquaintance with some of these plays. There are problems, though. Conventionally, it is supposed that many of us were bored by inept teaching: that Shakespeare was placed in a hollow, hallowed urn and revered as a great, or even worshipped, human being. It is thought that this prevented him and his work becoming part of the emotional fibre of our being. If this is true, it might be seen as inevitable, but I hope to show that there are better ways of teaching Shakespeare.

But in fact, according to many of my correspondents (I include their ages, in order to place their schooling roughly in the twentieth century) there was very little teaching of Shakespeare going on:

> I think I must have gone to Mr Gradgrind's school in Coke Town! We 'did' neither poetry nor Shakespeare at school. I was left to discover them for myself, for which I am grateful!…
>
> (aged 73)

> We didn't do any Shakespeare at all until 'O' level, when we did the Merchant and I played Antonio and the teacher had the effrontery to change the language…I didn't say 'In sooth I know not why I am so sad' but 'In truth…' One good thing he did was, he pointed out that because this was a boys' grammar school we had boys playing Portia and Jessica, and that was how it would have been in Shakespeare's time…
>
> And I remember the boy who played Portia, when he put his make-up on we all fell in love with him, he was gorgeous, we flocked around him…
>
> (aged 57)

Someone who had been taught Shakespeare (or who had 'done' him) recalls 'We had to learn "Once more unto the breach…" on pain of detention' (aged 53). Someone else recalls

> We did the Merchant when we were twelve. It seems an odd choice for a play at that age…I remember that it meant nothing to me….I first enjoyed Shakespeare when we were taken from school to the Vic [The Victoria Theatre in Stoke] to see The Tempest…
>
> (aged 43)

Ruston (1998) wrote to me

I wasn't taught any Shakespeare…before sixth form….I think my teacher deliberately chose not to expose us to Shakespeare. We read copiously – lots of those 60s northern writers such a Sillitoe, Hines, Barstow, Shelagh Delaney, Arnold Wesker; and a lot of poetry, such as Donne, Wilfred Owen, Stevie Smith, Ted Hughes, Robert Frost, Philip Larkin….However…I started reading Shakespeare of my own volition…The Dream…Later, in the sixth form, I was overwhelmed by the grandeur and enormity of *King Lear*…There were many, many theatre trips….Everything was casual…and I now look on those day as halcyon and wish my own students could enjoy literature in a less rigid, pressurized way…

(aged 39)

So despite any vague belief that Shakespeare is central to our natures, he has usually been kept to sixth forms, or, even, not taught at all. I hesitate to write this, but I think this is the first book written on Shakespeare and primary school children writing.

Depressingly, Shakespeare has often been seen as an elitist icon by progressive teachers. Neill, for example, is scornful and dismissive:

Summerhill children do not like dramatized stories. Nor do they want the usual highbrow stuff so common in other schools. Our crowd never acts Shakespeare; but sometimes I write a Shakespearean skit as, for example, *Julius Caesar* with an American gangster setting – the language a mixture of Shakespeare and a detective story magazine.

(1968: 71)

Many questions arise from this quotation, not all of them relevant to this book. One might ask though, about the phrase 'They do not like' – who asked them? Are Summerhill children really a particular kind of child, or just children who have arrived at the school for one or many of a million different reasons? 'Highbrow stuff' is exactly the sort of phrase that encapsulates the reasons for a thousand misinformed decisions about Shakespeare. Are the Porter's drunken greetings to his imaginary hellbound villains 'highbrow'? (see pp. 93–7) That word 'crowd' speaks volumes: phoney-democratic, unbearably matey; trying to argue a case in one syllable. We are a crowd, they are something less genial. 'I write': why didn't the children write? Didn't Neill have sufficient faith in the children's writing? Finally, how wonderfully dated is the phrase 'detective story magazine' compared with the word Shakespeare. Nothing, we know, is so out of date as recent fashions.

Among the most depressing stories I found about learning Shakespeare there comes the following from actors in Gilmour (1997: 73), who were presenting *Macbeth* to schoolchildren, and probably were not themselves very old. Indeed, as they refer to comprehensive schools, they were certainly of a generation younger by a few years than most of the correspondents quoted earlier.

One actor (Gilmour writes) described how, in the fourth year at secondary school, her class read *Romeo and Juliet*, their first Shakespeare play. It was a mixed comprehensive, but only the top set had to do Shakespeare. There was one book between three…Shakespeare became something that just had to be got through.

Another student remembered how they 'had to go through the whole text of a play from beginning to end, making notes and learning quotations for examinations'. Here is that cultural definition summed up. Shakespeare is 'done' at a certain stage for examinations. Even worse, he is 'gone through'. Enjoyment doesn't come into it. Nor does learning, really.

It is worth saying near the outset of my book that Shakespeare's greatness is not taken for granted. Shaw quaintly remarked that

> With the single exception of Homer, there is no eminent writer, not even Sir Walter Scott, whom I can despise so entirely as I despise Shakespeare when I measure my mind against his….It would positively be a relief to me to dig him up and throw stones at him.
>
> (Shaw 1907)

I note, though, that Professor Higgins in *Pygmalion* did not agree with his maker, and that Shaw himself said somewhere that the Countess in *All's Well That Ends Well* was the finest part for an older actress ever written. In any case, according to George Orwell, Shaw suffered 'from an inferiority complex towards Shakespeare' (quoted in Crick 1982). Darwin had no respect, either (1974). He was 'nauseated' by his dullness.

These opinions are not worth much, but Johnson's opinion is (if only because it discourages us from making a perfect, immaculate mystery of Shakespeare).

> Shakespeare never had six lines together without a fault. Perhaps you may find seven, but this does not refute my general assertion.
>
> (Boswell 1906: 24)

Such 'Grecian-urning' of him does neither him nor his young readers any favours, but fixes a dreadful gulf between them and his work. If there is one certain piece of advice to be given to a young teacher approaching Shakespeare in the primary classroom for the first time, it is this: *never tell the children that Shakespeare is the greatest writer that ever lived*. Never, in other words, make him a quasi-religious figure, an icon, a Grecian urn containing merely the beauty of unheard melodies. This attitude, combined with the fact that most children will inevitably, at first, find him difficult, is the surest of all turn-offs. The half-conscious thought process in the child goes something like this: 'So this is great? And I am baffled? There must be something wrong with me. I'll leave it alone'. I am reminded of a cartoon I saw once of two teenagers listening to a Beethoven symphony. They wore puzzled expressions, and one was saying 'I can't feel anything yet, can you?' It is the teacher's task to make sure that part of the cultural definition of Shakespeare – it is great, so therefore it will be a medicine or a drug to our souls – is crossed off the agenda as soon as we meet the children for the first lesson about *Romeo and Juliet*, or the *A Midsummer Night's Dream*, or *Macbeth*, or whatever play it is. Children should not study Shakespeare because of his greatness, but in spite of it. They should learn to ravish him.

Another equally serious and related problem is that there is in our culture a tendency towards an offensive sentimentalization of Shakespeare which disempowers his work. This is in spite of the way that the plays and poems demonstrate time and again how the sentimental and the vicious are closely linked. For example, Chiron in *Titus Andronicus* moves from his assertion 'I love Lavinia more than all the world' to an agreement to rape her together with his brother within three pages. The Prince of Wales, though, talks about 'the Bard' and his 'heritage', apparently ignorant of the reality of the moral implications of the plays and poems. To hear him speak, you'd think that the plays were only to do with elegance and nobility and our splendid English language and, by implication of course, a royal continuity. He seems to know nothing of the cowardliness of Sir John Falstaff, of the jealous wickedness of Iago, of the arrogant stupidity of Bottom, of the sexual fickleness of Troilus and Cressida, of what Ted Hughes (1992) calls the 'seedy philandering' of Bertram in *All's Well*; and is ignorant of the fact that these moral deficiencies are not always condemned by Shakespeare: see, especially, the way Falstaff's braggartly lying is positively celebrated in *Henry IV Part 1* so that we love the man, and we are moved to tears in *Henry V* when we hear the Hostess describe his death. Cotton says:

> Isn't this because *via* the plays we can, empathize with the essential humanity of the characters...understand that, indeed, human weakness may well be the essential stuff of our humanity. We are all redeemable....Our essential humanity redeems our weaknesses...
>
> (1998)

This thinking is a long way from 'Grecian-urning'. To sum up that cultural definition, we praise Shakespeare inordinately, we ignore him, we sentimentalize him. To re-apply a remark of Scannell's (1987) the successful teacher must love Shakespeare's words, but must not be a Shakespeare-lover. The child has to learn that 'Shakespeare is very good in spite of all the people who say he is very good' (Graves in Lamb 1992). It is better, I think, to see Shakespeare as 'that upstart crow' (his contemporary Robert Greene's bitter epithet) than as the 'Swan of Avon'.

Some problems

Preconceptions

This book, then, is based on case material of children aged between 5 and 14 enjoying Shakespeare (indeed, inspired by him) in their experiences as readers, and writers. In a sense, it began thirty-five years ago. Its first problem is that we all come to him, as teachers, with preconceptions. I met Sir John Falstaff some time in 1960 in a dull classroom in a South London grammar school:

FALSTAFF: Now Hal, what time of day is it, lad?
PRINCE: Thou art so fat-witted, with drinking of old sack, and unbuttoning thee after supper, and sleeping upon benches after noon, that thou hast forgotten to demand what truly thou would'st truly know…

(Henry IV Part I:I:2:1–9)

Then I saw John Stride as Prince Hal at the Old Vic (Tony Britton should have been Hotspur, but he had been injured the night before in a sword fight with Hal, and that heightened my new passion: they actually fought, and got hurt!). I don't remember who was Falstaff. I watched my little brother, then fourteen years old, play Gertrude at school to Hywel Bennett's Hamlet, potentially, I now reflect, a Freudian nightmare. Then, through my experiences as an enjoyer of Shakespeare, as an amateur actor, as a playgoer and occasional local radio critic, as a radio-listener, occasionally as a television-watcher, and as a reader, I have developed an enthusiasm that is really a passion.

I acted Second Servant at college in *King Lear*, watching Cornwall gouge out Gloucester's eyes. I had to pop little round capsules of red stuff against Gloucester's cheeks. My friend Richard (First Servant) had died in rehearsal like a starfish, flat on his back, horribly comic, until the director, the head of the English Department, showed him how stabbed people die ('Like this! They crumple!') He gripped his belly and twisted and squirmed to the ground. He lay there for a few seconds and looked up. 'Like that!' I have collected Hamlets (Olivier, of course, with his page boy hair-do); some bloke at OUDS seriously upstaged by Jonathan James-Moore as a Fascist Claudius; Ian McKellen, Michael Pennington, Martin Marquez (from *The Bill*). I have regretted missing others (especially Jonathan Pryce). I have, probably most importantly, puzzled over those love affairs in the Sonnets: that beautiful young man, that lady whose eyes 'are nothing like the sun'. I have laughed with and at Falstaff, recognizing, sometimes, elements of myself in him: 'I would it were bed-time, Hal, and all well'.

I include this account here to mirror whatever are my readers' preconceptions, and to emphasize that we have to recognize that the children we teach will bring different baggage to Shakespeare. They may open *A Midsummer Night's Dream*, for example, with a view of fairies that is quite at variance with the nature of Puck; culled, if they have been unlucky, from the appalling poems of Rose Fyleman as selected by the Opies (1973: 337) ('A fairy went a-marketing/She bought a little fish...')

Difficulty

A more serious problem than my preconceptions (I'll have to live with those, and try to change some of the prejudices they have led to) is the matter of the perceived difficulty of Shakespeare's work. This is, in large part, another preconception. I have been asked, while I've been writing this book, if I am using Shakespeare's language 'simplified'. When Rex Gibson asked primary school teachers if they had taught Shakespeare, one 'expressed surprise at my not realizing that "the language is right off the end of any known reading scale"' ('Shakespeare in Schools' no. 4, Autumn 1987). I have lost count of the times when teachers have said to me, 'I wrote a simplified version of A Midsummer Night's Dream (usually) or Macbeth (often) for the children and we produced it for the parents'. I have not found a polite way of asking, What's the point of this? Shakespeare is essentially his language. By comparison, his plots are almost incidental.

The language is often difficult, there can be no doubt. Coleridge wrote that he 'was not a whit more intelligible in his own day, except for a few local allusions of no consequence' (letter 1834). But this difficulty, as Gibson (1990) has put it, is 'an enabling difficulty...enjoyment increases with the sense of difficulties overcome'. And Shakespeare is also accessible because he is concerned with the human emotions and moral problems that we all share: importantly, his moral values reach us without the tiresome intrusion of moralizing. Of course, I have used his language as it has come to us in the Folio. I am stubborn in my insistence that the problem about the language is not essentially in that language, but in our preconceptions and expectations of it and in the children's reactions to it. Our own early difficulties, however many years ago, have bred prejudices in our practice with today's children. This is connected to two further points. First, if we must limit our children's experiences of language, are we going to choose 'reading scales' or are we going to choose Shakespeare? And second, this book is not just for teachers who are experts in Shakespeare's language, or in drama. I want to emphasize here that this book is for all primary teachers who are interested in education, whatever the experience of and prejudices about Shakespeare.

Yeats has a line about 'the fascination with what's difficult'. The fruit of that fascination may be there in our reading of a text, or in our writing one; or it may be in our immediate reflection on that text. But, in contrast, it may not appear and take hold of us for a long time. What is certain is that attention to the difficult will pay us back one day. Simone Weil writes: 'Even if our efforts of attention seem for years to be producing no result, one day a light that is exact proportion to them will flood the soul' (Panichas 1977: 29). Because of the certainty of that light, the difficulty of Shakespeare is part of the case for teaching it, not against. And attention to the perceived problems will make us readier to face other problems later on. For example, a study of *Romeo and Juliet* will help young people to face up to the imminent problems of love and sexuality. A reading of *King Lear* (with a reflection on the nothingness that is threaded throughout this play) will help us reflect on age and, more importantly, that great nil, that great emptiness that faces us from time to time like the stage in a play by Beckett, and the ripeness that is finally all. Gloucester makes explicit the educational function of literature and experience: these characters and readers 'learn about themselves', much as Heaney's school pupils write in order to 'fall into themselves unknowingly' ('The Play Way' in Heaney 1966: 56).

A common objection to Shakespeare in the primary school is that, because of its difficulty, it's best left to secondary years. I will leave the rebuttal of this confidently to the children and their poems. It is enough to quote here two of those children, one writing an over-the-top love poem in the light of Demetrius' lines in *A Midsummer Night's Dream* (III:2:137–144), and the other writing in terms of a lament from *Cymbeline* (IV:2:258–281). It's about time we heard the voices of children again, so I'll trail two of their poems here:

Oh dear beloved, your hair is darker
Than the night sky. Your lips are redder than
Blood. Let it touch my lips so to give life.
Your face is so beautiful and bright it
Makes the sun look black and flowers look ugly.
Your cheeks are redder than the reddest strawberry.
Your eyes are so golden and delightful
They make gold itself look cheap…

(Anon)

Fear no more the aiming from an arrow.
Fear no more the collar round your neck.
Fear no more the feeling of following humans.
Fear no more the rain and no shelter.

(Anon)

There are two problems that are particular to the project described in this book, both of which teachers can avoid. Gibson (1998) says that commitment to Shakespeare should be such that a class will be involved in a play for a significant period of time – say a term, or at least half a term. But, because of the nature of my work, this has never been possible for me. I travel from school to school, and it isn't unusual for me to be in Peterlee, Durham, on a Monday and a Tuesday, and in Ipswich, Suffolk, or Stevenage, Hertfordshire on the same week's Thursday or Friday. Therefore, any long term commitment depends on the teachers in the school: I am not personally committed to any one play with any one group of children. There is a second problem connected with this and, because my concern is with children writing, it is more important. Almost all the poems and other writings given in this book are either first or second drafts: there was only rarely a chance to give children time and teaching to enable them to see how much further work would improve their writing. These occasions were when I was a resident in a school for a longer period.

The improper

Shakespeare's plays are riddled throughout, like life for most of us – the lucky ones anyway – with the unrespectable, the questionable, the improper. Sometimes in the plays we stand in the palace, but often we loiter in the street, the tavern or even the brothel. The first scene of *Romeo and Juliet* is practically based on what used to be called indecency. 'To be valiant is to stand', of course, but not only in one sense of the word 'stand'. The weak 'go to the wall', but for more than one reason. Heads are heads, but also maidenheads. Sampson is 'a pretty piece of flesh', and when Gregory cries 'Draw thy tool', we know which piece of his flesh Sampson thinks is the prettiest. Indeed, Sampson's weapon is 'naked' and 'fear me not' he will not 'turn [his] back and run'. Later, Mercutio teases Romeo with what Amis called, in a different context (1954), a 'brief manic flurry of' obscenity (II:1:17–38). As Partridge (1948: 45) says, 'Mercutio and the Nurse sex-spatter the most lyrically tragic of the plays'.

And yet this is the pretty piece deemed proper by prissy politicians to be taught first, in contrast to modern plays with all their sex and violence. One wonders, with Seymour-Smith (1975: 373) 'what the intellectually hapless Mrs Whitehouse would have to say about *Measure for Measure*', with *Othello*, the 'most sexual, most bawdy play' (Partridge); or *Henry V*:455–8, where Shakespeare slyly uses what Hughes (1998: 107) calls 'the ultimate taboos in French'. Anyone wanting to take on more of the fascinating subject of Shakespeare's obscenity is directed to Hughes and, of course, Partridge (1948).

I spoke to one teacher who had taught *Romeo and Juliet* to her class, and she made a face when I told her about how 'rude' much of Shakespeare's dialogue was. She didn't believe me, and hadn't read the play recently, merely a version of the plot. Another teacher, Ruston, told me:

> I was teaching this to a C stream, and when I read 'Draw thy tool' a boy sniggered and I said to him, that's right, every time you hear the word 'tool' in Shakespeare you should look for dirty meaning....You can use Shakespeare to subvert the Government's thinking here...the children got to the point where they loved Shakespeare...
>
> (1998)

This vulgarity is so evident to even a casual reader that a sound and potentially very successful way to introduce Shakespeare's plays and poems to younger readers would be to compile an anthology of all his most disreputable bits. My next project is *Shakespeare's Filth for Schools*, a sort of Bowdler in reverse. It will begin with Malvolio reading the letter that Maria has sent to him (*Twelfth Night* II:5:72–79).[1]

An early introduction to Shakespeare's bawdy would lead to a greater commitment to and enjoyment of the work in adult life. Even in many of the parts of Shakespeare's plays that are most accessible to younger students, the songs, we have ribaldry. An apparently innocent number in *The Winter's Tale*, for example, goes:

> When daffodils begin to peer,
>   With heigh! the doxy, over the dale,
> Why, then comes in the sweet o' the year;
>   For the red blood reigns in the winter's pale.
>
> The white sheet bleaching on the hedge,
>   With heigh! the sweet birds, O, how they sing!
> Does set my pugging tooth on edge;
>   For a quart of ale is a dish for king.
>
> The lark, that tirra-lirra chants,
>   With heigh, with heigh, the thrush and the jay,
> Are summer songs for me and my aunts,
>   While we lie tumbling in the hay.
>
>   (IV:3:1–12)

Pafford, in his edition of the play, tells us that 'doxy' means 'beggar's girl', and that 'aunt' has a similar meaning. But SOED has nothing of this, locating a usage from 1678 as 'procuress' or 'prostitute', and Partridge tells us that it means 'a paramour in general, or even a wanton'. In any case, this is not the innocent song of a bard from some sentimentally recalled Merrie England, which is roughly how politicians see Shakespeare. His use of bawdy was (Seymour-Smith 1975: 373) 'considerable, extensive and acceptable to his audience'.

But I cannot pretend that Shakespeare's bawdy didn't present me, as I collected children's writing for this book, with a large difficulty. While I felt I

---

1   Certainly, my Latin would be better today had I not been force-fed Caesar's Gallic War, but instead encouraged to read Martial's scabrous, sexy, lavatorial, insulting epigrams; for example, 'In the baths':

> That shout from the shallow end:
> Big Mac's exposing (not *again!*)
> His bestest, bestest, bestest friend.

                                                           (translated by Emily Roeves)

could get away with the Porter's speech in *Macbeth* (II:3), I was sure that his subsequent lines about the three things that drink provokes ('nose-painting, sleep, and urine. Lechery, sir, it provokes and unprovokes...') would have got me into trouble in most schools had I continued that far in the scene. And yet my stance throughout this book is anti-censorship; positively libertarian, if I'm pushed; certainly in favour of the thorough teaching of Shakespeare's lowest scenes. As I write, I am consciously looking for a school where I feel I might be able to teach lines such as this. The reader will be able to tell from the main part of the book whether I have found any such schools. Writers in Gilmour (1997: 36) took a different line from mine '[removing]...anything that was coarse or bawdy' from *The Tempest*. To me this is like taking the mustard from a hot dog or the froth from a pint of beer: it removed a certain element of zest.

Finally, John Cotton tells me a story:

> We went to Sam Wannamaker's Globe...A superb production of *As You Like It*....What was interesting, following our debate on how much we do leave out, from embarrassment, censorship or whatever, when we present Shakespeare in school. A large part of the audience was from what you might call a posh girls' school – all blue blazers and white blouses....I wondered what they made of it, especially the teachers, as the production provided plenty of bawdy stuff. Emphasis was placed on the 'country copulatives'....Did the young ladies expect all that when they read the play in the classroom? I am sure their education was enhanced by a few notches, but would everyone agree?

> (1998)

Tales: the post-Lamb tradition

Even modern narrative accounts go for the codpiece and flounces view of Shakespeare, all that 'Beauty of the Bard' stuff instead of *Shakespeare as Our Contemporary* (title of Jan Kott's book). I have in front of me some narrative versions of the plays. Geraldine McCaughrean's *Stories from Shakespeare* is an example. After a sonnet, the real *Romeo and Juliet* opens with the barrage of *double entendre* that I have described above. What does McCaughrean give us in place of this life, this poetry and this street-ribaldry? It is certainly different: 'Once, in a sweltering Italian city named Verona, one man wronged another. It does not matter who wronged whom or how....' Thus the focus is taken away from Shakespeare's here and now, and placed on prosy family history.

Again, Hamlet famously opens in the middle of the drama:

> ...Who's there?...Nay answer me: stand and unfold yourself....Long live the king!...Bernardo?...He....You come most carefully upon your hour....'Tis now struck twelve; get thee to bed, Francisco...

> (I:1:1–7)

In contrast, McCaughrean writes, 'There was once a castle full of shadows…', neutralizing the shock of Shakespeare's opening, and making her own conventional.

There are versions of Shakespeare's plays illustrated by Eric Kincaid and published by Brimax, that, wisely, do not offer a story-teller's name. 'He immediately felt a great surge of love, and quickly told her so…' is a typical sentence. The illustrations depict every kind of relevant stereotype: Oberon with a helmet made of fairy's wings, Titania a sleeping robed beauty, the fairies naughty fellows swinging from willow branches. In Brimax's account of *The Tempest*, Miranda wears courtly robes even though she had never seen a court, and the Caliban, mostly ape, would be incapable of any human speech, let alone the lovely lines he does say: 'I'll show thee the best springs; I'll pluck thee berries;/I'll fish for thee, and get thee wood enough…//I prithee let me bring thee where crabs grow;/And I with my long nails will dig thee pignuts…' (II:2:146–54).

While Shakespeare's play hits us in the middle of the drama:

MASTER: Boatswain!

BOATSWAIN: Here, master. What cheer?

MASTER: Good; speak to th'mariners. Fall to't yarely, or we run ourselves aground. Bestir, bestir!

(I:1:1–4)

Brimax gives us dull prose. These books are offered to us as ways of introducing children to Shakespeare's work. Even Leon Garfield's muscular versions, with Michael Foreman's excellent illustrations, miss the point. Being in prose, they've (obviously) lost the poetry. Surprisingly, the otherwise excellent Peel (1971: 132) shoves Shakespeare's language to the side in favour of the plots (though Shakespeare merely stole other men's plots and *Holinshed's Chronicles* – and made them live) and a study of the history of Elizabethan theatre. This latter approach has become common with the arrival of the national curriculum, which, as I write, includes Shakespeare's theatre in Key Stage 2 in History, but ignores him in English. When Peel does suggest the examination of a play, *The Merchant of Venice*, she suggests 'not starting from the original but from a good retelling such as Ian Serraillier…or Charles and Mary Lamb…' which is missing the whole point.

These ways of sticking Shakespeare to a moment in our history, to a role as literary representative to a royal dynasty, or to a set of values that is now out of date, belie the fact that every generation has to reinvent Shakespeare for itself. To take the most dramatic example: Michael Billington tells us that

> modern scholarship and theatrical practice see Bassanio [in *The Merchant of Venice*] as either a fortune-hunting opportunist or a man agonizingly torn between his new wife and his old male lover. We live in a post-Freudian,

post-Holocaust world; you cannot turn the clock back and present [this play] as a play untouched by history'.

(1998)

Exactly. You cannot teach it outside that history either. Shylock the Jew in the Lambs' account is a stereotype that has taken on much greater offensiveness in our century. While the Lambs see the play as an account of Good (the merchant and his friends) versus Evil (Shylock the Jew) we know now as well as we know anything that this will not do. Other casual references to the Jews mean something profoundly different to us compared with what they meant to Shakepeare and his contemporaries. In *The Two Gentlemen of Verona*, Launce, describing his hard-hearted dog, Crab, says that 'a Jew would have wept' at something that left Crab unmoved, hinting at a stereotype of Jews now largely forgotten in favour of other stereotypes. This is all to show, once again, that Shakespeare's work is not the simple matter of 'great language' and 'our heritage' that politicians take it for, and that we must not rely on narrative accounts of the stories.

Dover Wilson (1949: xiii) tells a tale that those of us who sum Shakespeare up entirely in terms of his plots should note well. There is a story called *Amleth* written by Saxo Grammaticus. It dates from the end of the twelfth century. In this story we have a wicked uncle who has killed his brother-king, and married his widow, and a threatened nephew who plays the fool while seeking revenge; we have a girl to whom the hero is attracted but does not marry, and who is used as a bait by the King and his friend to lure Amleth from his disguised madness. Amleth kills the King's friend ('he drove his sword into the spot and impaled him who lay hid')....The reader can guess the rest. Only the Ghost and the travelling players are missing from *Amleth*. The plot of *Hamlet* is practically irrelevant to Shakespeare's genius and our teaching of his works to children.

To sum up: this book is about children's and Shakespeare's words, and the effect those words can have on children's writing. It has an emphasis on the text that necessarily rejects any sentimentalization of the bard. It sees children as active learners – 'players' is the happy word that comes to mind with all its punning possibilities – who will learn through their enjoyment of Shakespeare, and their responding to his work mostly, though not entirely, through their own writing; who will look into the glass he has set up for them, and therein see their inmost parts, and the inmost parts of the world they live in, with its grandeur and its squalor, with its palaces and its taverns, with its boudoirs and its brothels.

Chapter 1

Mouth full of news

Single lines and single speeches

I am concerned in this book first, with children learning about Shakespeare's poetry and prose. Second, it is concerned with children using that poetry and prose to learn about the world they live in. Third, it is concerned with children learning about their own natures *via* the technique of writing in the grip of Shakespeare's words.

There is one point I would like to have developed further. I mention it here briefly, and hope to return to it at another time and in another place. As adults – teachers, parents, grandparents, governors, classroom assistants – we can all learn in that exhilarating, uncomfortable grip, and I think adult learning is implicit in everything I am saying; that it can, therefore, be inferred from every exercise in the book. Some of the best sessions with children happened when their teacher spent some of the time writing. Such an activity implicitly taught the children something about writing – its importance, the fact that it goes on beyond childhood, that it is not a matter of words coming by magic after we've said 'Shazam!' (Graves 1983: 43) – that no amount of preaching could teach. But I have neither the space nor the remit to present and discuss case studies on the adult learning that has taken place on courses, the poems that have been written by teachers.

Certainly I have learned more and more about Shakespeare myself and language as I have studied the plays and poems again, cheating occasionally with a vibrant, surprising anthology (Hughes 1998) and even a dictionary of quotations that, at times, feels like an anthology (Lamb 1992). The most intensive learning for me has come from re-reading the Sonnets with the help of Helen Vendler's extraordinary new edition (1997).

But I return to my current priority, the child/Shakespeare relationship. In a sense, this book is also about enabling children to produce parts of the plays in their own heads. When, for example, we read Puck's words in A *Midsummer Night's Dream* with anything like due attention, we can sense his physical movement in, or through, them, and we should be able to help children to sense those movements – though differently. (See p. 46 for an example of a speech through which Puck moves.) These mental productions cannot be mounted without the words, so they present a contrast to practice in one school I visited. The 'brightest' group in Year-6 had (I was told) studied *A Midsummer Night's Dream*, the middle group *Romeo and Juliet* and the least able *Macbeth*. How this decision was made is not recorded. Why Puck, Bottom, Titania and friends are deemed more appropriate to clever children, and Lady Macbeth ('Unsex me here') more appropriate to the...shall we say, least clever, is hard to see. Perhaps the brightest are the most fanciful, the middle groups most likely to fall in love tragically, and the dimmest (the word has been hovering for ages, I might as well use it, it is what's in the minds of the teachers and managers concerned) most likely to murder people and become kings and queens.

Also, the children had studied the plays with no copies of the texts. As one teacher said, without irony, 'It wasn't easy'. The children had merely been taught the stories in the plays, looked at some of the characters as mediated through the teachers' accounts, and written prose descriptions of those characters, and little narratives of events. There was no evident faith and hope in the children on the part of the teachers that would have allowed the children to play with Shakespeare's words. There was no evident love of those words.

Reader, actor, critic, writer

The first way of learning about these words is to read them and think about them. This is the way of the private reader. He or she may, in his or her mind, concentrate on the poetry, or may emphasize moving the characters around the stage in terms of a perfect production. His or her method may be a combination of these two. The second way is to read them and then act them. This is the way of the amateur actor, in school, or college or in the dramatic society; or (rarely, of course, in the experience of the children we teach) professionally. Obviously, this way involves learning the words by heart, or, more accurately, by rote learning, which we will discuss in Chapter 7. The third way of learning about the words is to think about them, or see them acted, and then write about them. This is the way of the critic. The fourth way is to write in imitation of them. That is what the children represented in this book have done. A study of Shakespeare's words, leading to a lifelong engagement with them can, I suggest, be at least in part achieved by writing in homage to those words. A child who has written down four or five times in her own poem Puck's line 'Now it is the time of night' will probably never forget that line.

Before going on to the examples that I have collected, I would like to draw the reader's attention to the work of Cathy Carter and Ian Douglas (Carter 1997: 70–6). The insights their ten and eleven-year-olds achieved after an intensive study of *Hamlet* are enough to knock aside any argument about suitability for primary children, or simplified language. One child said about Polonius's relationship to his children 'He has brought them up not to behave badly, but he puts them in awkward positions, like when he tells Ophelia she couldn't see Hamlet again'. The next stage in perception will probably be when this child notices the even worse position Ophelia is put in by the King and her father, when she 'loosed' to Hamlet, and is foully insulted by him. Other children in the Clwyd Project that generated this work reflected on Gertrude's line 'Good Hamlet, cast thy nighted colour off' and one child wrote, as Hamlet, '…there's a trumpet playing a hard/and dark song in my mind'. Another child, 'preoccupied with that idea of "the undiscover'd country" [wrote] "I may be in that lost bit of the world"'.

The children also made paintings inspired by *Hamlet*: 'Ophelia drowning in Hamlet's sea of troubles and King Hamlet [sitting] against a tree in a garden that is already unweeded [while] his brother Claudius is one of the things "rank and gross in nature" sweeping down from a tree as a serpent'. Readers are directed toward Carter's book for a fuller account of this project, and colour reproductions of the dramatic paintings.

Single lines

With his mouth full of news

This section really belongs with other writing developed from *As You Like It* (see Chapter 3), but I have put it here because it represents a toe-wetting, utterly painless experience in beginning Shakespeare: early play. Children, far from needing to study the whole text, can study single scenes or speeches. Indeed, one might profitably take this a stage or two further. To look at one vivid line has two happy effects: first, it takes much of the perceived threat out of Shakespeare (both for the children and, I found in the early days of this project, for me), and second, it concentrates the mind on the matter in hand: the words and their relationships to one another. Here are some young writers studying one such short line – indeed, it is only a half line – and in doing so learning more about Shakespeare's methods than they would learn by trying to swallow merely the plot through a whole scene, let alone a whole act, or a whole play.

Celia says in *As You Like It*: 'Here comes Monsieur Le Beau' and Rosalind replies 'With his mouth full of news' (I:2: 85–6). Later, Celia describes Duke Frederick coming 'with his eyes full of anger' (I:3:36). And hurriedly a class of children write, at first rather literally, and with no deeper knowledge of the play (that will come later):

> With his mouth full of tongue
>
> with his mouth full of teeth
>
> with his ears full of wax
>
> with his eyes full of eyeballs

But soon they loosen up:

With his ears full of lies

with his eyes full of tears

with his brain full of stupidity

with his heart full of love...

with her mouth full of songs

with his mouth full of gossip

with his eye full of fire

with her hands full of gold

Later, the teacher asked them to do the same exercise with an animal:

with her eyes full of night

with his nose full of another dog

with his heart full of rage

with his belly full of hunger...

One writer composed this impressive list on her own:

With his ears full of gossip

With his eyes full of love

With his heart full of sorrow

With her lips full of treasure (teeth)

With her smile full of wickedness

With his knuckles red with anger

With his body full of excitement

With her face full of merriment

With her cheeks rosy with laughter

With his lips full of hate

With his heart full of sorrow

(Natasha, 11)

I read to Natasha and her friends the lines that surround the anger reference:

ROSALIND: Look, here comes the Duke.
CELIA: With his eyes full of anger.
DUKE: Mistress, dispatch you with your safest haste
    And get you from our court.
ROSALIND: Me uncle?
DUKE: You cousin…

(I:2:35–41)

We acted these lines in various characterizations. Rosalind was, by turns, fearful, cheeky and insolent; Celia was satirical, anxious and neutral. Then I asked the children to choose one of their lines, and continue the dialogue. Natasha wrote:

He said, with his eyes full of sorrow,
I will be executed the day after next
& lie without my head at the Tower of London

To write in this formula is to be set free to write in a fresh way, and to learn something about Shakespeare's method – in particular the way a character says something about another character coming on stage, and the way Shakespeare mixes the abstract (anger and news) with the concrete (mouth and eyes). Shakespeare here is the teacher; the children, too, mix the abstract and the concrete. Also, the fact that these two similar half-lines occur so close together in the play tells us as readers of the play something about the nature of the relationship between Celia and Rosalind: they are so close that there are habits in their speech that are common to each other, and they have elements of the same sense of humour.

As You Like It is dotted with little lines that get children going: Orlando talks about going 'from the smoke into the smother' (I:2:227) – clearly an extinct version of our frying pan/fire saying, and when Celia asks Rosalind if she has 'not a word', Rosalind replies 'Not one to throw at a dog' (I:3:3). The children quoted next have listened to several sayings like this, and then written their own. In doing so, they are playing at the heart of demotic English, partly because (once again) they are mixing concrete and abstract, and partly because such sayings, while rooted in experience, are not clichés:

From my garden to my neighbour's

From the wheelie-bin to the dustbin lorry

From the teacher to the headmaster

These examples might seem ordinary. Then the same children offered:

From life to death

Can you add to those words? I said to the child who'd written that line, and he wrote:

From my life to my death

Then

From Heaven into Hell

From meat into salad

From God into the Devil

Other lines written were:

I haven't a thought to fly in the sky

...a dream to call my own

...a draft to work on

* * *

I wrote a line from *Antony and Cleopatra* (III:13:20–1) on the board, and we said it a few times: 'He wears the rose/Of youth upon him'

She wears a bud of babyhood on her

He wears the dead daffodil of age upon him

Those two were mine, as I was playing with the idea the night before. I didn't read them to the children. I'm glad to say they did far better:

He wipes the dust of innocence off his shirt.
                                    (Sarelle, 10)

She dries the wet peachy face of eighteen births off her.
                                    (Nikki, 9)

She lets out the glow of human sunshine around her.
                                    (Lizbeth, 11)

He carries the tattered robe of earth with him.
                                    (Adam, 11)

He carries the oaktree of age in his mind.

(Daniel, 10)

I carry the golden hour upon my back.

(Melissa, 9)

He drags the thorny bush of spite behind him.

(Anna, 10)

Half way through the lesson, I reminded the children about alliteration. They hit a new note in their writing almost effortlessly:

He wears the weed of weakness about him.

He flies the flag of fame in his hand.

(Douglas, 9)

He wears the red rose of romance at his daughter's wedding.

(Daniel, 9)

'The dust of innocence'; 'the wet peachy face of eighteen births'; 'the tattered robe of earth'; 'the oaktree of age'; 'the thorny bush of spite'; 'the weed of weakness': some of these phrases, among other more conventional ones, had a startling ring to them, a genuine freshness. We played with another line, this time prose, where Falstaff, exhausted in the battle at Shrewsbury, says: 'I am as hot as molten lead, and as heavy too' (*I Henry IV*: V:3:32).

I am as cold as glass, and as breakable.
I am bright as a streetlamp, but less useful.

Again, the first two were mine. And again, the children did better. I suspect that our insultingly low expectations of what children can achieve (made solid, as those dreary expectations are in statutory levels, targets, objectives and the like) are really expectations of our own potential. We are subconsciously envious of what children can do, and therefore in our minds, we drag them down to our own level, the level of those who are no longer trailing clouds of glory, and certain of nothing except the holiness of the heart's affection and the truth of the imagination, but numbed into cliché and predictability.

I am as silent and slender as sunshine and as lovely too.

(Anna, 10)

I am as hot as glass against the sun and as bright too.

(Sarah, 10)

I am as ticklish as a feather and as light too.

(Emily, 9)

I am as dry as a funeral drum but not as dark.

(Daniel, 10)

We played with Prospero's promise to Ariel: 'Thou shalt be free/As mountain winds' (*The Tempest* I:2:498–9). One boy wrote 'Thou shalt be trapped as dreams waiting to be told'. Throughout this lesson, we had the company of a sixteen-year-old girl from a comprehensive school, there on work experience, and she showed us that she was still trailing those clouds of Wordsworth's: 'It was as lost as yesterday, and as forgotten too....She was as alone as the world, and as empty, too...'

The stars, I see, will kiss the valleys first: Two examples from *The Winter's Tale*

In this play there are many lines that serve the purpose of demonstrating elements of Shakespeare's method. The plot hardly touches children's experience in any way that makes telling the story worthwhile. Leontes has what appears to be a nervous breakdown in the first act, and accuses his innocent best friend and his innocent wife of adultery. There is a wonderful resolution in forgiveness and repentance. But children do appreciate the powerful, hyperbolic rhetorical device used by Camillo when he expresses his belief that something is unlikely to happen; that, in fact, the 'fabric' of Leontes jealous 'folly' about his wife and Polixenes will be 'shaken': '...you may as well' he says 'Forbid the sea for to obey the moon...' (I:2:426–7). And later, expressing disbelief that he and Perdita will ever marry (a result, years later, of Leontes' folly) Florizel says: 'The stars, I see, will kiss the valleys first' (V:1:205).

Children in a forty-strong group in a small village school divided themselves, with the teacher's help, into pairs composed of one older child (nine years and above) and one younger one (nine and below) and we talked about impossible things that, however impossible they were, were, in fact, more likely than something else. 'I'm more likely to fly' I said, lamely' 'than find a school cloakroom without coats all over the floor'. Then, warming to my theme (if not improving much) 'Those freckles will move from Alison's face/To John's before the world is fair and true...' I wrote the lines from *The Winter's Tale* at the front of the classroom, and we counted syllables – first in the children's names ('Kath – er – in – a Lear...Mal – colm Mac-beth...Ro – sa – lind La – few') and then in the lines. We spoke the words several times to get the feel of two things: first, the length of an iambic pentameter, and second its rhythm. The children wrote their own lines, working in their twosomes:

The ivy will grow up to the sky and
grow round the sun.

This one resulted from an older child complaining that she and her partner couldn't get her line into one pentameter: we simply made it one and a half. This came in handy with this example:

Fish will lose their scales and get tangled in
Fisherman's nets and seaweed.

The dictionary will turn into nonsense.

Then I talked about alliteration, and the lines came again, with a renewed vigour and, one more, a little extra music:

Rain will wreck the rotation of the earth.

The great great giants will pull the great sun down.

The sun will swim backstrokes in the sea.

Mountains will migrate to Jamaica
for the winter.

Metre sticks will measure the years.

The last one (two syllables short, of course) reminded me of a line of Eliot's 'Prufrock': 'I have measured out my life with coffee spoons'. I have noticed before how an element of luck informs children's writing, and their teachers' reaction to it.

The fluffy fluffy clouds turn into thunder.

This one demonstrates an easy way of getting the right number of syllables: repeat a word until all is as you want it.

Computers will cry over the Crimean war.

Lions will lose their manes and sink into the sunset.

The windy weather will fall into the water.

I don't want to give the wrong impression that iambic pentameters are merely a matter of counting syllables. As Stillman (1966) explains, 'pent' means five

[feet] and the 'iamb' means a two-syllable foot with the accent on the second syllable. Thus

The stars, I see, will kiss the valleys first

is a near-perfect example. But it is possible to use counting syllables to make children aware of line lengths; and then to help them go on to subtler work. And indeed, the children in this short session began, after an hour, to use accurate iambic pentameters. It is certainly more effective to teach this by saying the Shakespeare lines aloud with feeling and sensitivity to the meaning several times, thus allowing the iambic beat to sink into the brain, than to count drably: 'te-tum te-tum te-tum te-tum te-tum'.

In *The Winter's Tale* there is a sad character, a little boy, the son of Leontes and Hermione. Mamillius is praised by everyone who meets him, and he is much loved by his parents. We learn, however, as the tragedy takes hold, that Mamillius has died in childhood. At one point his mother asks him to tell her a story, and he begins:

There was a man [he is interrupted by his mother] dwelt by a churchyard...
(II:1:28–30)

and that is as far as his story goes. I asked a class of nine to eleven-year-olds to complete the story, using exactly fifty words, and not worrying about bringing the story to a conclusion. In other words, it should leave some questions unanswered.

There was a man dwelt by a churchyard. He was sad. He slept on graves. He didn't have a name. He could only read the Bible and say prayers. The townspeople thought he was weird but saw him everyday. Sunday morning he was found crying and trying to bury himself.

(Anna, 10)

There was a man dwelt by a churchyard who lived hundreds of years ago and lived a good life like a king but one day he heard people plotting against him so he jumped out of the window and fled to a shady place under a willow.

(Melissa, 10)

Other stories produced lines that were part of what Larkin once called the 'myth kitty' of our thinking, as though the line from *The Winter's Tale* was somehow basic to us all: 'he had all the things in the world but no friends'; 'he had everything, gold, silver, wine, long purple robes'. Other stories produced oddities – lines that I felt sure had never been written before: 'In his house he had some long curly steps' was one example.

Other single lines

Other lines that children could use from plays by Shakespeare include the following. If we have faith in them – both the children and the lines – the writers will surprise us.

> Out of this nettle, danger, we pluck this flower, safety
> >(*I Henry IV*:II:3:8)

> A horse! A horse! My kingdom for a horse!
> >(*Richard III*:V:4:7)

> Uneasy lies the head that wears a crown
> >(*I Henry IV*:III:1:31)

Single speeches

A structure from **A Comedy of Errors**

We can, of course, look beyond the individual line to the structure of a speech, or a part of one. In *A Comedy of Errors* Dromio of Ephesus tells his master that he is late for dinner:

> …the meat is cold.
> The meat is cold because you come not home.
> You come not home because you have no stomach.
> You have no stomach, having broke your fast…
> >(I:2:47–52)

This is a comic structure that Shakespeare found useful in this early play. He was still playing with his craft, and children, writing their own early works, and, of course playing with them, find it useful too. Children readily act this little speech, repeating each phrase and then adding their own. One boy had been making cakes in an earlier lesson, and wrote this:

> When I mixed the flour and butter I added the salt.
> When I added the salt I added the eggs.
> When I added the eggs, I got a mixture.
> When I got a mixture, I added the sugar.
> When I added the sugar, I poured it in the moulds.
> When I poured it in the moulds, I put it in the oven.
> When I put it in the oven, it started to bake.
> When it started to bake, I mixed water and colouring.
> When I mixed water and colouring, I mixed in icing sugar.

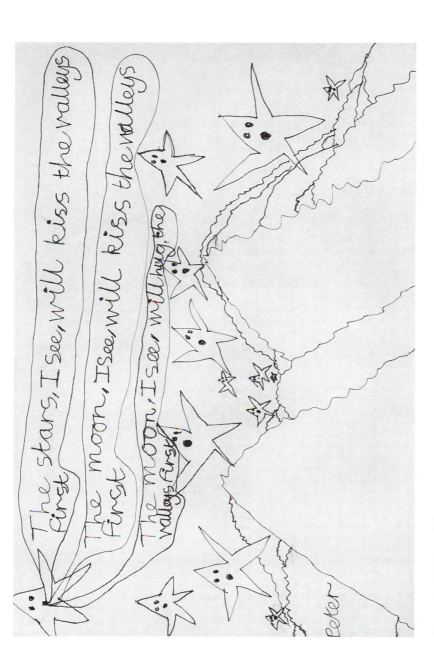

Illustration I Peter (7)

When I mixed in icing sugar, the mixture had baked.
When the mixture had baked, I took them out.
When I took them out, I put on the icing.
When I put on the icing, I left them to cool.
When I left them to cool, I got out the sprinkles.
When I got out the sprinkles, the cakes had cooled.
When the cakes had cooled, I poured on the sprinkles.
When I poured on the sprinkles, the cakes were ready.
When the cakes were ready, I ate them for tea.

(Richard, 10)

Children report events using this technique:

When the alarm clock didn't go off my father didn't wake up
when my father didn't wake up he went on snoring
when he went on snoring he woke me up
when I woke up it was very very late
when it was very very late I didn't bother with breakfast
when I didn't bother with breakfast I starved at school...

(Henry, 8)

and explore the emotional causes of their actions, and the active causes of emotions:

I sulked because she'd gone off on her own.
She'd gone off on her own because I had told her she wasn't my best friend any more.
I had told her she wasn't my best friend any more because she didn't phone last night
She didn't phone last night...

(Ameline, 10)

These pieces are less dramatic than the ones quoted earlier which were derived from single lines; but they are valuable because they show children playing with a technique that is new to them, and which sets them free.

Once more unto the breach dear friends

Another better known speech is one that a correspondent of mine remembers learning by heart on pain of detention: 'Once more unto the breach, dear friends, once more...'. It continues

Or close the wall up with our English dead.
In peace there's nothing so becomes a man

As modest stillness and humility;
But when the blast of war blows in our ears,
Then imitate the action of the tiger;
Stiffen the sinews, conjure up the blood...

(*Henry V* III:1:1–7)

I said these famous words to a small group of children on a Pearse House course, and asked them how they might rouse an army for victory. I asked them about the images that Henry uses, and they quickly identified the animals, the eyes and the face in general. We discussed the strange pictures here: the eyes peering through portholes, the eyebrows like an outcrop of rock over a cliff. We talked about what Henry is trying to do in order to rouse his troops.

Some of the children drew the image in these lines

Then lend the eye a terrible aspect.
Let it pry through them portage of the head
Like the brass cannon; let the brow o'erwhelm it
As fearfully as doth a galled rock
O'erhang and jutty his confounded base...

(*Henry V* III:1:9–13)

And then wrote their own militaristic speeches

Once more unto the breach, dear friends, once more...
Don't be like a mouse and hold back in fear.
Pierce their evils hearts using your piercing eyes.
Go forward and fight them, do not be shy.
If you have courage, if you have wit,
Show off to the world and fight for us now.
Do you care for us? Show it now.
Save us from death, hurt and destruction.
Be like a volcano, explode and bury them.
Show us what you are made of, and fight for us now.

(Rosie, 10)

I did not feel that this work was very successful. Indeed, Rosie's is the only vital piece that was written in this session, and I didn't try the idea again. I had taught this lesson very early in the research for this book, and reflected later that the children (or I) may perhaps have had less empathy with the military triumphalism of the speech than we might have with other kingly words in Shakespeare. Another session from another history play suggests I may be right. *Richard II* has powerful speeches that stimulate children to write, and I wondered what I might find here to help children.

Shakespeare has an obsession with the results of disorder, especially in this play and also in *Troilus and Cressida*: 'The heavens themselves, the planets, and this centre/Observe degree, priority, and place...' (I:3:85–6). In *Richard II*, a Welsh soldier describes the results of the chaos caused by the people's assumption that the King is dead

> 'Tis thought the King is dead; we will not stay.
> The bay trees in our country are all withered,
> And meteors fright the fixed stars of heaven,
> The pale-faced moon looks bloody on the earth,
> And lean-looked prophets whisper fearful change;
> Rich men look sad, and ruffians dance and leap...
>
> (II:4:7–12)

I read the children these lines, and also Adrian Henri's famous poem, 'Tonight at Noon' (in Patten (ed.) 1991: 106), and they wrote lines describing things that might happen when 'the times are out of joint':

> The teachers know nothing. Vicars preach evil
> From their pulpits...
>
> (Jasmine, 10)

> Skinny men run restaurants and say, Come in and eat.
> Get fat like me...
>
> (Rahima, 10)

> The sun rains storms. The moon burns people.
> The rainbow means another storm, another cloud opening.
> The snow scalds my skin. The wind will settle
> on my rabbit's fur and it will lie still...
>
> (Maria, 10)

I did this activity again, with more time, in a class of nine- and ten-year olds. They were 'not very bright', I was told. Nervously I began with a more straightforward and familiar (to me, anyway) activity, *The Box*, from Sedgwick (1997: 44). Then, once the children had limbered up mentally and emotionally, I told them about the withered bay trees, the meteors, the bloody moon, the lean-looked prophets, the sad rich men and the dancing ruffians. When they began to write, I noticed many spelling problems, but few problems, if any, with grasping the essence of the message. I print some of the work here as it was written, so that the gap between mechanical correctness (important, no doubt to a society training hired hands to work its systems) and imaginative flexibility (important to a different kind of society) can be seen.

All bildings turn to water.
Peoples sols [souls] fly about in the dark black sky.
all the rich and famous people turn poor and lay on the streets for years to
diy.
evry one turns angry and all over the world people fight and steele
all over the world people turn nasty and bad and even from space you can
see the nastyness.
prinsess diana comes out of her grave
and honrts the peple that hav been
nasty to her in the past
posters come alive.
dung betels rule the world.
The powet and teacher disaper from my classroom in the middle of a leson
doors get stuck and the world stops sining.

(Joyce, 10)

mony turns to dust as you try to pay.
books turn to slime as you pick one up.
clothes turn to hair as you put them on.
your hair turns to rock as you brush it.
your blood turn to milk as you do a oparation.
clocks stope as you look at the time.
your walls begin to leak with blood.
people begin to eat their tungs.
as you get married goasts return…

(Kylie, 10)

The sand will come up
over the water.

At noon in the night
mice will hunt owls.

Tomorrow come yesterday
gravity will expel planets
deeper into space.

Tomorrow come yesterday
God will dissolve us
into the sky.

Yesterday come tomorrow
the clock in the hall
will read
half-past twenty

and in the evening of tomorrow morning
reality will be
woken up by the dead.

Tomorrow come yesterday
elephants will be stamped down
by the jungle.

Tomorrow come yesterday
hatred will be loved by love.
Yesterday come tomorrow
the sea will dry up the sun

and in the dawn of tomorrow evening
elephants will erode away
and cliffs will be fat and grey.

Tomorrow come yesterday
cats will talk to us
and we will be sitting helplessly
listening.

(Amy, 10)

'Even from space you can see the nastyness…mony turns to dust as you try to
pay…as you get married goasts return.…' To appreciate the nervy acuity of
these lines, and to show that appreciation, is more important educationally
than to bemoan the unconventional spelling and punctuation. As Harold
Rosen once said to Donald Graves 'Any idiot can tell a genius he's made a
spelling mistake' (Graves 1983: 188). Anyone intent on marking rather than
appreciation will miss the learning going on in these poems. In the third
example, the child passes the conventional spelling test and writes with vigour
and originality as well.

Later, the King describes the lack of order from his point of view as he
prepares to hand over kingship to Henry Bolingbroke. These must be some of
the saddest lines in any of the plays.

I'll give my jewels/for a set of beads;
My gorgeous palace/for a hermitage;
My gay apparel/for an almsman's gown;
My figured goblets/for a dish of wood;
My sceptre/for a palmer's walking-staff;
My subjects/for a pair of carved saints;
And my large kingdom/for a little grave
A little, little grave,/an obscure grave…

(III:3:146–53)

Case studies later in this book will make clear how opposites are typical of Shakespeare's work: *Romeo and Juliet* especially is rich in oxymorons, and *Macbeth* too uses paradox: 'So foul and fair a day I have not seen'. More generally, if we teach a child to write, after hearing lines like 'jewels for a set of beads...gorgeous palace for a hermitage' that are composed of contrasts – and contrasts in particular that are about downfall – he or she is learning much about one of Shakespeare's many methods. Also the children who studied these lines learned about the caesura in the iambic pentameter (the 'break in the flow of sound within a line caused by a break in meaning' according to Stillman 1966: 24) because it is especially clear in these lines – I have marked it with obliques in the quotation above. As the children learned the speech, I taught them to change their way of speaking at each caesura. For example, they said the first halves of the lines strongly, the second halves weakly; or the first halves in a high register, the second halves in a low one. They also shared each line between two voices.

I asked them to imagine being brought low, and losing all kinds of riches – not just pecuniary ones. Then they wrote

> I'll give my tennis court up for a broken racket.
> my black Mercedes for a broken bicycle.
> I swap my four poster bed for a tiny sack,
> my large typewriter for a small notepad.
> I'll give my golden bath for a little water jug,
> my clothes for a tiny ripped dress.
> I'll swap my orchestra for an untuned piano.

(Naomi, 10)

> I'll give my lunch for a grain of wheat
> I'll give my light for a candle
> I'll exchange my bedroom for a no-star flat
> my whole wood for a dead sycamore
> and even my whole range of books
> for a small black leather-bound Bible.

(Douglas, 10)

Douglas has imitated Shakespeare's dying fall: compare 'A little, little grave, an obscure grave...' with his final lines. The next writer has picked up 'obscure' usefully from Shakespeare

> I'll give my house up for a tiny shed.
> I'll give my friends up for an obscure photo
> I'll exchange my computer for a piece of paper and a pencil.
> I'll give up playing to sit in a dark room everyday.
> I'll lend my bed for a centimetre of wood
> my life for the strength of an ant.

I'll swap my mind for an ant's brain and my toys for dust.

(Nichaesha, 10)

I felt, as I hinted above, that the children were more at home with the personality in these lines than they were with the personality in 'Once more unto the
breach'. Richard's lines are intensely and sadly human and of course sincere;
Henry's lines are political in the sense that they are designed to whip up feeling.
The images in Richard's lines are relatively simple, as well: there is no difficulty
visualizing the jewels and the beads, the gorgeous palace and the hermitage, the
gay apparel and the almsman's gown. I, for one, cannot say the same for 'the
portage of the head' and 'the brow o'erwhelm[ing] it'. The clarity of much of
Shakespeare's imagery became a touchstone for many of the examples I chose in
writing this book. First of all, A *Midsummer Night's Dream* is full of clear pictures
that children respond to.

Chapter 2

Now it is the time of night
A Midsummer Night's Dream

What is the magic of this play? One correspondent suggested to me that it isn't a good one for children today because of 'all that fairy stuff', but I have found that children enjoy all the parts of it I have shared with them. They are drawn to it, first, because it is full of mischief. They often use the word 'wicked' to mean 'good', and, as I have written elsewhere, any writing ideas that legitimate wickedness have a head start on others. I suggested children might write poems entirely composed of lies about objects in my earlier book (1997: 99) with the support of Picasso, who says somewhere that art is a lie told to tell the truth. In my book I suggest that young writers attempt poems that are made up of boasts. Children attack these tasks with a relish similar to the enjoyment with which they first encounter Puck, whose mischief is, in some ways, like their own.

A second reason for the power of A Midsummer Night's Dream is the magic itself. The play is, in fact, as Philippa Pearce (1992: 75) says an early example of what is today called 'Magical Realism'. The fairies represent an ethereal, pastoral world that many children fantasize about when they are safely but dully shut up in bed. The first act moves easily and convincingly from a formal, rather cold statement about wedding plans to a domestic crisis (Egeus' complaint against his daughter). It then depicts unrequited love; we meet some absurd working class actors, and finally, the magic is suddenly and unexpectedly (if we are coming to the play for the first time) announced at II:1:1, as Puck says to another fairy: 'How now, spirit, whither wander you?'

Third, some of the characters in A Midsummer Night's Dream are so childlike that children reading the lines, I suggest, unconsciously recognize themselves. In III:1 the clowns – Bottom, Quince, Starveling, Snug and Flute – meet to plan their play within the play ('A tedious brief scene of young Pyramus/And his love Thisbe, very tragical mirth'). They sound like nothing so much as a group of infants planning a game: 'I'll be the mother and you be the sister...' The worries Starveling has ('I believe we must leave the killing out, when all is done....I fear it, I promise you') are expressed like a child's worries, and so are Bottom's easy, brash solutions: 'I have a device to make all well'; and so is his hyperactive, irrepressible enthusiasm: 'A calendar, a calendar! Look in the almanac – find out moonshine, find out moonshine!' Later, when they perform the play in front of the nobility, the clowns are exposed as children, and patron-ized by their superiors – their teachers, in my analogy – especially Theseus: 'This wall, methinks, being sensible, should curse again'. Bottom (V:1:180) even answers back: 'No, in truth, he should not'.

Lines in Shakespeare often contain one powerful figure of speech that is missed when we study the whole play, or even a whole scene. The first page of *A Midsummer Night's Dream* has a simile that is potent in the classroom for teaching about the language itself, and about similes in general. Hyppolyta anticipates her wedding ceremonies ('solemnities') to her husband-to-be and others with a clear image of the new moon.

> Four days will quickly steep themselves in night;
> Four nights will quickly dream away the time;
> And then the moon, like to a silver bow
> New bent in heaven, shall behold the night
> Of our solemnities.
>
> (I:1:9–10)

I read these lines to a group of forty children, and then divided them into four groups. Each group spoke in unison one of the half lines from 'And then the moon...' to '...behold the night'. We experimented by saying the words in different ways: mysterious, matter of fact, threatening. This is important because it works against the notion that there is only one way to say and, by extension, produce or act Shakespeare. After I had chosen the ways of speaking the lines, different children took turns to be leaders. We changed each group's words three times, so that everyone had a go at each half line. We discussed the simile of the moon 'like to a silver bow', and acted it, making mimes of a hunter caught in the act of punching the middle of the crescent moon outwards, while pulling back the ends of it with the strings of his bow. What similes could the children suggest for the sun, the stars and the dark?

> and then the sun like to a golden flame
> and then sun like a dazzling light
> and then the sun like a ball of burning gas
>
> and then the stars like a dazzling magical night
> and then the stars like a sparkling firework night
> and then the stars like little fireflies
>
> and then the dark like to the skin of a bat flying in the midnight sky
> and then the dark like to a grim reaper
> and then the dark like as black as dark coal

Other children wrote:

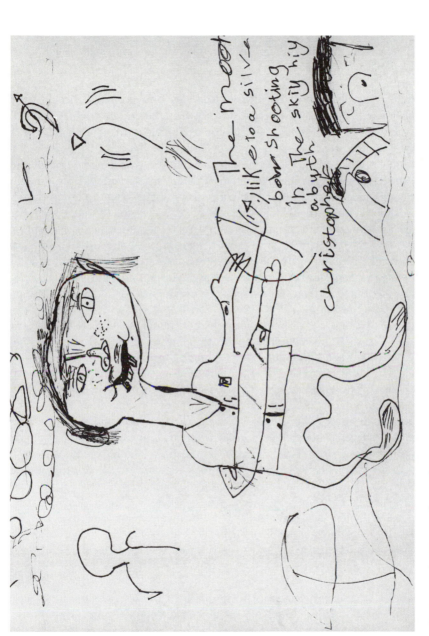

Illustration 2 Christopher (7)

the stars like glitter in the distance…like sparks of the past…like spoons shining away in the night…eating away at the darkness…shimmering in the night sky doing nothing…the dark like a mist in a cave…like a spider's legs…like to a black badger…like black boots stomping…like the inside of a black box…like a creeping panther…like the hair on a spider's legs…like ashy coal…

While some of the children's first ideas are conventional ('glitter in the distance', for example), as they continued to write the children achieved freshness. 'The sun like to a golden flame', for example, is almost a cliché, but it helps the same writer to move towards 'and then the dark like to the skin of a bat' which is more original and, to my ears, quasi-Shakespearean. This phrase has required a jump of the imagination from dark – as seen, presumably, through a bedroom window – to a bat seen flitting in the night, or in a natural history book. This writer had stretched her concepts of darkness and of simile under the force of Shakespeare's line. Young writers always bring something to the writing lesson, and while it might seem to us as teachers to be conventional, it might lead to words and phrases that are fresher. Also, what is conventional to us as experienced readers (the same writer's 'grim reaper' for example) is not necessarily conventional to them. Here, a child is playing with a cliché and learning about it and its meaning.

Names are central to our humanity. Why else would Adam have labelled the creatures so early in his relationship with them? Why else do we think so hard before deciding what to call our children, and often resent so strongly what we are called by our parents? The most explicit linking of creativity and nomenclature is the lovely sentence 'Imagination is the ability to name cats' (Auden, after Samuel Butler in *The Dyer's Hand* – a title itself named from Shakespeare and quoted in Brownjohn 1989). Of course, history sometimes imposed on Shakespeare his characters' titles, and stories he had inherited did the same. At other times what characters are called is significant in a more pointed way: both Angelo's superficial goodness and his deep wickedness are called into question by his name. Caliban is almost an anagram for 'cannibal'.

Shakespeare's fairies are, of course, Puck, Oberon, Titania, Peaseblossom, Cobweb, Moth and Mustardseed. The following examples are five, six and seven-year-old children re-naming Puck. They didn't, at this stage, know his real name, or, interestingly, given the fourth example, any of the characters in *A Midsummer Night's Dream*:

Cheery fairy. Egg-head. Fish. Bottom. Pooh. Rubbish. Featherhead. Peg. Pickle. Bully Fairy. Mischief. Troublemaker. Flit. Rudy. Norty-bortie. Naughty Nancy Nickletoes. Zombie.

I read the same children some of Puck's lines describing what he does (see pp. 45–6 below) and they wrote down some of the things a 'naughty fairy' might do:

The fairy pulled someone's pants down. He put a spell and some kind of stuff into someone's eyes. When someone was asleep he put a spell into someone's mouth and made the people on his side.

The naughty fairy
creeped up behind a man
and hit him
on the back

He made someone really silly
with his magic

The naughty fairy
put a plastic sock
in someones eye

The fairy showed off He said Im going to be a horse a hound and a bear I will neigh and woof and grrrrr wot a naughty fairy.

Jamie's writing is special. It says:

mischeif
mac fund and litrh
rund crash e and rudb

and underneath the teacher has written:

Thunder and lightning
Rumble! Crash together!

It is important to me because Miss has also written: 'special needs; this is his third piece of unaided writing'. This has at least three messages. First, although this teacher's motives were entirely honourable (she wanted this boy's achievement to be appreciated and, indeed, celebrated, for something like what it was), 'special needs' has become almost as strong a label that 'dunce', 'backward' or 'remedial' once were in their different times. Second, Shakespeare's words have released in this boy, however he is perceived by his teachers, a neat poem. Third, I would question whether writing a conventional version of his words underneath helped his confidence. Why not make sure we know what he is saying, and then publish it to everyone with the correct amount of praise and encouragement?

One writer on a Pearse House course invented new fairies to add to Peaseblossom and the others 'got carried away with the idea' (Cotton 1998) and 'produced some ten flower fairies all based on the character of the flowers themselves…'.

Four fairies

Daffodil

She wears a big poke-bonnet
which shades her pale face
from the sun.
Her hair is like the celandine's
but she wears it
outside her bonnet.
Being tall she can see a lot
from her positions and loves
to sing softly to herself
at night.

Celandine

Her glossy fair hair
glints in the sun
and she wears a waxy
green cap at the back
of her head. The pale green
centre of her bright
yellow face is small and
round as it grins
at you walking by.

Dandylion

He has a golden face
with matching hair
and a little green
hat like a bell.
When the sun shines
he reflects it.
But when it rains
he hides beneath
his hat.
He is always chatting
to his neighbours.

Foxgloves

They line up as though in school
on a green stalk and are taught

by trees, the wind
and older flowers.
They have pink poke bonnets
trimmed with white silk
and with black and white
spotted linings.
They have different characters
and ginger hair.

(Alison, 11)

Here is an example of a writer taking the initial stimulus of the fairies in *A Midsummer Night's Dream* from her teacher, and then mixing it with at least two pieces of old information – those fairy flower books ubiquitous in remainder shops, and her knowledge of wild flowers. She demonstrates a truth about education: it is not merely about taking in the new, a relatively passive exercise, but about assimilating the new with the already known – a much more active, complex and interesting affair. The writing charms by its idiosyncrasy, some of it, maybe, fortuitous: the alliteration in the second poem ('glossy...glints...green...grins') and the neatly appropriate line endings. The writer has, evidently, just discovered poke bonnets and they mean a lot to her. The foxgloves 'lining up as though in school' is neat. It is even neater when Alison extends the school idea in the lines that follow: 'are taught/by trees, the wind/and older flowers...'). The poems seem to own a similar fragile delicacy to the flowers.

I have suggested that single lines provide an approach in which the teacher and child, in the process of reflective reading, can let the context grow around the line organically. We can also use names, and groups of lines. The next step is to use whole speeches with children. Shakespeare's language is not always difficult, as we can see from the next example.

There are several ways of introducing Puck. First, he introduces himself with:

I am that merry wanderer of the night.
I jest to Oberon, and make him smile
When I a fat and bean-fed horse beguile,
Neighing in likeness of a filly foal;
And sometimes lurk I in a gossip's bowl
In very likeness of a roasted crab,
And when she drinks, against her lips I bob,
And on her weathered dewlap pour the ale...

(II:143)

I talked to a group of eight and nine-year-olds about the mischievous things they would do if they were such 'merry wanderers'. This presented them with no problems. As I've written earlier, asking children to write about mischief, or, more exactly, in terms of it, is almost always a good stimulus. There was another sense of play here: first, of course, we are dealing with *plays*, we are teaching children *playing* with words, and now the children are writing about mischievous *play*.

> I am that merry wanderer
> I kick the stars out of place and ruin constellations
> I scare teachers by moving the chalk …
> I pretend to be an octopus in a lake and when people are swimming
> I tangle up with their legs
>
> > (Jonathan, 8)

> I am that lonely tourist
> that is going to pull the stars and moon
> out of the sky
> to make the sky black as ebony …
> I pull stings out of bumble bees …
>
> > (Emma, 8)

These two examples were among the most Puckian, and they also caught the flavour of the whole play. Some writers used the idea to take little revenges. Excerpts from other poems were:

> I put scorpions on teachers' bellies when they are sunbathing…I put my studded boots on and stamp on the carpet…I sharpen my pencil on girls' heads and rub the rubber on teachers' feet just to tickle them…
>
> > (Isaac, 8)

Then I read some of Puck's lines to the children. In this jerky, angular speech we get a clear sense of Puck's movement as well as his behaviour.

> I'll follow you: I'll lead about a round,
>   Through bog, through bush, through brake, through briar;
> Sometime a horse I'll be, sometime a hound,
>   A hog, a headless bear, sometime a fire,
> And neigh, and bark, and grunt, and roar, and burn,
> Like horse, hound, hog, bear, fire at every turn.
>
> > (III:1 87–94)

I pointed out how staccato the words are: short phrases and sentences that enact Puck's movements through the forest. I demonstrated this movement with my hand. These rapid half-lines are another reason why Puck appeals to children, apart from his mischief, he is never convoluted in his speech. And I was struck by how children, like Puck, are quick. Watching them run out to

Illustration 3 Puck changing into fire: Darcelan (7)

play in another school, I thought of Puck at line 100 of III:2: 'I go, I go, look how I go!...'. Puck's words, like his sense of mischief, mirror the alert and occasionally subversive enthusiasms of childhood. I also pointed out to the children that the speech doesn't always say what we, with our modern ears, might expect it to say: it has 'about a round' instead of 'a roundabout' and 'sometime' for 'sometimes'.

The children said the speech after me, to underline its style. And then, although we were in a classroom full of tables and chairs, we found just enough room to act the lines, calling them out as we walked, ran, or dodged around our imaginary wood, looking up to the ceiling and down to the floor, staring into the imaginary distance and reacting appropriately to the faces looming suddenly over us, or leering up at us. We looked out at the building site on which was about to rise the children's new school (the present one had been condemned); we also talked briefly about supermarkets and town centres. And the children wrote their versions of the speech, putting it in a new urban setting. I was pleased that nearly all of them chose very short lines to emphasize the jerky movement. I am typing here the first poem as carefully as I can to show how the writer wrote it.

> I'll follow you
> through the bushes
> through the trees
> through the flowers
> with the bees.
> I'll follow you
> through dark and night
> through the mud
> all through the night.
> I'll follow you
> through ice and snow.
> I'll follow high
> I'll follow low.
> I'll follow you
> through the bushes
> through the trees
> through the flowers
> with the bees.

(Claire, 9)

We have to take our responsibility as readers of poems by children seriously. This means paying as much attention as the child seems to need. We need to respond to each piece of writing as we would to a poem in a book that we want to understand and gain pleasure from. We have, in other words, to behave like serious readers, or even critics. If this leads us occasionally to read too much into something a child has written, that is a small price to pay for the encouragement the child will receive from our attention. And we have another reason for this alertness when responding to children's writing: we have to try to identify what learning is going on in the writing process, so that we can reflect on our practice and make it better.

These poems, when we respond to them as active readers, speak to us about something that is essentially educational. By this I mean that they are not concerned with closing things down. They don't trap the writer in a way of thinking – they open out further possibilities. They don't limit the writer to one way of responding – they make the response unpredictable. They are not stale worksheets to which there is only one response – they leave in the air the possibility of freshness, of a brand new sentence that has never been uttered before in the whole history of the human race. As Gibson (1988) puts it, Shakespeare's words have 'emancipatory possibilities'.

Children have too much difficulty in rhyming to make it a worthwhile fetish in the classroom. They appear not to have been born, as Benedick says he wasn't in *Much Ado About Nothing* (V:2) 'under a rhyming planet'. They are, on the other hand, good at alliteration and assonance. But here, although Claire rhymes 'night' with itself, she achieves an appropriate effect with the rest of the rhymes. Even though they are conventional, they seem to haunt the reader, just as the speaker threatens to haunt her quarry. The structure enhances this effect, suggesting that the words and the lines, like the speaker, will go anywhere required in the chase.

Another child wrote:

> I'll follow you
> through sand
> over and under
> through sea
> beneath and between
> through trees
> through and above
> through torture
> around and away
> through heaven
> through hell
> through hatred
> I'll follow you
> The way you go
> I've already been...

> (Ben, 9)

Almost all the poems children wrote during this session moved from the physical ('sand', 'sea', 'bushes', 'flowers', 'mud' and 'trees') to the abstract ('heaven', 'hell' and 'hatred') because while the front of the mind (represented more clearly in the beginning of the poem) works on something relatively graspable, the back of it (which is represented more clearly towards the end of the poem) goes, often unconsciously, deeper. The more these child-writers worked, the more they went beyond the observable into the hidden. Learning that this was so was learning an important lesson for all creative writers; indeed, for all artists.

Romaine's poem reminded me of a song by the Police: 'Every breath you take' (1983), which was widely mis-read as a simple love song. In fact, it is a scary little piece about extreme jealousy, and one day I will use it with Puck's speech while teaching children to write. Perhaps Romaine's parents had the song in their collection at home, and the writer had absorbed it subconsciously over the years of her childhood, and allowed it to seep into her head as she wrote. Writing depends to some extent at least on luck, and the quiet, gradual impact of rhythms, tunes and words we are not always aware of hearing. In any case, the hidden material here is striking.

> I'll follow you
> through trolleys,
> through people
> and children.
> I'll follow you
> around aisles,
> food and drink.
> I'll follow you
> everywhere you go
> every corner,
> every wall,
> everywhere I'll be.
> I'll follow you
> in every room
> every place
> no matter where.
> I'll follow you
> I'll hold on to every word,
> every sentence
> every conversation you have.
> I'll follow you
> everything you see I see
> everything you do I do
> everything you say I'll hear
> I'll be there.

(Romaine, 9)

Talking about this poem afterwards with the teachers in the school, several of us found it disturbing – like the Police song. It moves from being an exercise about the supermarket, using the Puck speech, to being a poem (is Romaine conscious of this or not?) about an obsessive follower. Is this what the Puck speech is essentially about?

One writer used the adjacent building site: 'Through unfinished buildings/over tree stumps/and under railings/round the vehicles/through the rain…' and another poem became very strange, developing like Romaine's, and leaving trees and rivers behind: '...round sorrow, guilt and betrayal I'll follow you...' Another child used rhyme with unusual neatness: 'I'll follow you/down under ground/where worms wriggle with no sound/where moles feed, where beetles are found...' and then abandoned it in her unusual ending: 'I'll follow you in your house where you wash and eat and sleep and get visitors...'

We can see here how Shakespeare's words, far from being distant and irrelevant to today's child-writers, are 'the source of meaning and significance for each generation' (Gibson 1990). He treats all emotions: love, hate, fear, anxiety, jealousy; and he is concerned, too, with politics. Through Puck's words, Romaine and the other children reflect on something that seems to be very modern: obsessive stalking. In other places in this book, we can see children engaging with themes relevant to their lives more effectively than they might through some fustian 'life skills' programme.

I was keen to see how infants would respond to the same Shakespeare speech, and I tried it out at the first opportunity that arose. There was no thought in my mind of 'simplifying' the language when I started. I read the speech much as I had done to the juniors previously, and then got the children saying the speech after me. We were in a school's open-plan quiet room, where we could not act the speech, as some of the juniors had done.

> I follow you
> I follow you in school
> I follow you in your house
> I follow you in your sleep
> I follow you in the distance
> I follow you in the trees
> I follow you in the mirror
> I follow you in the mountains
> I follow you over the sun
> I follow you at night
> I follow you in the day
>
> (Charlotte, 6)

There is, of course, a random quality about this writing. It is less sophisticated in structure than the work done by the more mature writers, and Charlotte was less open to hints I dropped to both groups about varying the repetition of the central phrase. But how much more fluent it is than writing done for less honourable motives: a bald account of the whole plot, for example, done to show any passing inspectors that *A Midsummer Night's Dream* had been taught or (as people say) 'done'. How much more affection (passion) there is in it than there is in such accounts; how authentically it speaks: both of a child's life, and of a sudden, unexpected engagement with some words of Shakespeare's. I have used this speech many times now, changing my technique slightly each time, and it has never failed to help the children produce memorable writing.

Sometimes we collect other words close to 'follow' in meaning. The children
offer 'pursue', 'sneak after', 'chase' and others, and this varies the final products.

The songs are ways into the plays for many of us. 'Master William
Shakespeare' is, after all, 'that sweet Songster and Nurse of Wit and Humour'
according to Mother Goose's Melody, published in 1760 (quoted by Styles 1998:
188). I have used many songs from the plays with children. I read some children
the fairies' lullaby in A Midsummer Night's Dream.

> You spotted snakes with double tongue,
>   Thorny hedgehogs, be not seen.
> Newts and blindworms, do no wrong,
>   Come not near our Fairy Queen...
>
> Weaving spiders, come not here;
>   Hence, you long-legged spinners, hence!
> Beetles black approach not near;
>   Worm nor snail, do no offence...
>
>   (II:2:9–30)

I asked the children for some features of the song: what do you notice
happens in this poem? I admit that I acted it up, and the children came up
readily with the repetitions, the soft sounds, the gentle assonance. It's a truism
to say that teaching and acting are not as distinct as people suppose. No-one
who hates being in front of children will make a good teacher, however much
he or she believes (as I do) that the most creative place isn't, as a rule, in front
of them, but alongside them. Anyway, after the teacher's acting (or hamming
up) came the children's poems. Could the children make a lullaby for themselves, or for a friend they were fond of, or for a little brother or sister? The first
time I did this I was with a Pearse House group of keen writers aged between
nine and eleven, and they took up the challenge enthusiastically and, in Ruth's
case especially, with more knowledge of words than I might have expected:

> Do not feel vulnerable my friend
> The lightning will not strike you
> The hail will not tear your soul
> So rest and sleep.
>
> Do not fear for you are a trap,
> Images will fade at the edge of your boundary
> They will be struck by fear themselves.
> The sun will comfort you in your troubles.
> Understand you are the most delicate,
> No-one hears your footsteps,
> Do not fear, sleep.

The ululating wind will not disturb you
An eagle will swoop and not see you
A fox will prowl but not smell you
You are safe, rest.

Do not fear for you are a trap,
Images will fade at the edge of your boundary
They will be struck by fear themselves.
The sun will comfort you in your troubles.
Understand you are the most delicate,
No-one hears your footsteps,
Do not fear, sleep.

(Ruth, 11)

'An eagle will swoop and not see you/A fox will prowl but not smell you' is very mature writing, suggesting other influences: the Authorized Version of the Bible, perhaps? Similarly, 'Images will fade at the edge of your boundary/They will be struck by fear themselves' is a subtle depiction of the most appropriate end for wicked predators. The repetition of these lines, suggested, of course, by the fairies' song, added to the impact of this poem. Lines like this will surprise only those whose expectations of children are conditioned by a deficit model of what they cannot do, and by a politically-motivated obsession with statistics. Another poem read:

Lullaby sweet lullaby
no lawnmower shall pass you by
no shredder shall cut you
but flowers will keep you safe.

Lullaby sweet lullaby
no hiccuping loud music or sudden sounds
for we shall protect you throughout
especially from cats strolling around.

You will sleep without a whisper
even a murmur won't be found
beneath the earth and bumpy ground
little ants shall not be weeping.
They will be in happiness
that you are just sleeping.
Lullaby lullaby
nothing shall pass our queen by.

(Emma, 9)

'Hiccuping' in the first draft had been crossed out, and replaced with something much more conventional – I forget what – and I counselled the retention of the original word.

> Go to sleep
> Now
> Bats and bees stay away,
> Leave our fairy Queen in peace
> For she has done nothing to harm you
>
> Humans please stay away,
> Lizards, creepy-crawlies,
> Please leave the Queen alone
> The Queen alone.
> Go to sleep
> Now
>
> Go to sleep
> Now
> No gnomes are to come near
> As we are the fairies' guards.
> Shoo wasp...

> (Vicky, 11)

Infants faced with the same challenge wrote very differently – and, in the first example, with a pleasing bizarreness. But this time, I don't think they wrote with any less effect.

> Harowing raptor
> Oh harowing raptor gulp please don't come near me With your shiny snapping juicy teeth and your sharp claws Oh you make me so frightened that I run away very very fast.
>
> Harowing sharks
> Oh harowing sharks please don't some near me in the sea with your sharp puffing teeth or I will get very very scared
>
> Harowing Cheter
> Oh harowing cheeter please don't make me climb on your back because if you go fast you will make me sick.

> (Tushil, 7)

> Oh wasps
> you black and yellow wasps
> dont sting me
> oh spider

dont spin a web round me
oh whale
dont lay on me
oh burglars
dont steal from me
oh robots
you grey robots
dont crush me
oh ghosts you white ghosts
dont take me to your castle

(Carl, 6)

Oh skeleton
don't come near me
with your broken bones
and your yellow teeth.
Oh robots
don't touch me
with your cold metal hands.
and your horrible faces.
with colourful teeth.
Oh scary wolf
don't eat me
with your snappy sharp teeth.
Oh Labrador dogs
don't lick me
with your cold blue tongues.

(Rachel, 7)

I think all three of these poems show achievements that infants sometimes find easier than juniors. First, there is an organic structure. I have printed all three of these pieces here exactly as they were written. The boys show up an old truth: that what very young children write resembles poetry naturally more than it resembles fiction even though teachers have gone on and on for generations about writing 'stories', whether the children were telling news, reporting on a nature walk or a science experiment or, indeed, writing a story. Carl and Tushil repeat words inside their structures appropriately: 'Oh wasps/you black and yellow wasps...' for example. Second, these writers are not afraid of obscurity: 'Oh harowing raptor gulp...' means almost nothing to me (and it meant almost nothing to the teacher, too) but it was simply right for this boy, and he stuck to it. His poem may well be evidence of the influence of comics or even video games. His concentration as he wrote was awesome to watch – he held his pencil like a knife, and scored the graphite marks into the paper. He rarely wrote at any length normally, his teacher told me, and the teacher was impressed by what Shakespeare had achieved here as a teacher himself. Rachel's poem also has a kind of obscurity ('colourful teeth…cold blue tongues…') that I think gives it resonance.

Another time, using the idea of lullabies, I would quote to the children Imogen's goodnight prayer from *Cymbeline*: 'To your protection, I commend me, gods,/From fairies and from tempters of the night,/Guard me, beseech ye!' (II:2:8–10).

Writing about love

If thou remember'st not the slightest folly
That ever love did make thee run into,
Thou hast not loved.
Or if thou hast not sat as I do now,
Wearying thy hearer in thy mistress' praise,
Thou hast not loved.
Or if thou hast not broke from company
Abruptly as my passion now makes me,
Thou hast not loved.

(*As You Like It* II:4:31–9)

Teachers need to have greater faith and hope in their children and themselves than is required in current government thinking. They also need to love more: love their material, love the children. I will make this more explicit in my conclusion. It is enough to say here that love is a constant theme throughout this book. Children will, as they grow up, come across many different kinds of love. Most of us like to pretend, at given times in our lives, that the only love we have known, and that the children are likely to know, is 'true love'. But we face a few facts on dark nights: one is that, as Billie Holiday's song says, there is 'love for sale'. We know too that there is unrequited love. There is desperate love, like Silvius' love in the speech quoted at the head of this section. All adults have known, and will admit if they are honest, that there are loves that exaggerate themselves for various purposes.

Shakespeare's plays are disturbing teachers about love. In *Hamlet* alone, there is the Prince's furious, obscene complexity ('Do you think I meant country matters?') that drives Ophelia to madness; Gertrude's and 'bloat' Claudius' 'seamy…wanton…reechy' kisses; and the playful, and ultimately poignant love of brother and sister for each other. An example children appreciate is in III:2 of *A Midsummer Night's Dream*. In the forest during that enchanted night, Demetrius wakes. Puck has poured the love potion into his eyes. Demetrius sees Helena who, up to now, had been the despised girl; of course, he falls violently in love with her. This is a kind of love, though I wouldn't call it true love.

O Helen, goddess, nymph, perfect, divine!
To what, my love, shall I compare thine eyne?
Crystal is muddy! O, how ripe in show
Thy lips, those kissing cherries, tempting grow!...

(III:2:137–44)

I read, or rather acted – indeed hammed up, once again – these over-heated lines. I asked the children if the lines sounded sincere. They felt, more or less unanimously, that they weren't. They said they were 'posh', 'untrue', 'lies'. I asked them to write 'an over-the-top' love poem about anyone they liked: a film star or pop singer to name two suggested examples. I asked them not to write about someone they really loved, because the exaggerated quality required would have struck a potentially disastrous false note.

Some of the writers, understandably, came up with clichés: 'Your lips are redder than the first bud on a rose bush' was one example. One child wrote a love poem addressed to me: 'Your glasses are like blocks of ice/Your nose is like a strawberry'. But the same writer who wrote the bud/rose/bush line also, minutes later, managed 'My eyes have set upon you like a bird', which has, to my ears at least, an exemplary, delicate violence: imagine those feathers (gentle) and those claws with their sharpness. And look at that word 'set': accurate and frightening. We all bring to writing a personal baggage: perhaps mine here noticeably includes a viewing of Hitchcock's film *The Birds*.

Another young writer wrote this, playing with dangerous and seductive ideas:

You are a god to me
Silver is worthless compared to you.
Your eyes are like the sun perfect in every way.
Your hair is like the rolling waves swept over your brow.
Your skin is softer than a peach.
Your smile is sweeter than the sweetest smelling rose.
I would trek miles just to see your perfectly formed nose.
You smell sweeter than the most expensive fragrance.
Your touch is softer than the most softest thing in the world.
I couldn't bear to lose you
You are my heaven and earth

(Nikki, 10)

Here is the complete poem written by the child who had managed the beautiful bird line:

Oh you beautiful god of pure love.
My eyes have set upon you like a bird
Your hair is as soft as the first dawn in May.

Your lips are redder than the first bud in a rose bush.
Your cheeks are as flushed as a
person who is looking for only pure love.
Rubies are no contest for your heavenly eyes
You speak the finest breath heaven can make.
Your nose is as soft as cotton wool
fresh from the cotton flower.
When our eyes meet I only hope your soft
blinks can be heard by a new butterfly
When your hands hold
mine I only hope it can be love for me.
In my dreams only you can be found tampering in my mind.
The clear blue sea is no definition of my love to you.

(John, 12)

A hint of the rhyme in Shakespeare's words survives in Nikki's poem: 'Your smile is sweeter than the sweetest smelling rose/I would trek miles just to see your perfectly formed nose'. This serves well the tone of banality required by one interpretation of the setting, and for once legitimizes a kind of rhyme that mostly we as teachers are usually very superior about. Teachers are also superior about usages like 'most softest'. But Shakespeare does this: there is, for example, the 'most unkindest cut of all' in *Julius Caesar*. Likewise, Shakespeare mixes metaphors when he needs to. Taking 'arms against a sea of troubles', as Hamlet does, seems an even more impossible task because of the irregular usage. Shakespeare teaches us here not to be pedantic about grammar: it serves us, we are not supposed to serve it. There is a striking use of hyperbole ('I only hope your soft blinks can be heard by a new butterfly'). One line was, indisputably, a new sentence: surely what all writers are aiming for: 'In my dreams only you can be found tampering in my mind'.

With another group, I took the activity further. I asked them to write that overheated love speech, and then offer poor tormented Helena's response to it:

Oh dear beloved, your hair is darker
Than the night sky. Your lips are redder than
Blood. Let it touch my lips so to give life.
Your face is so beautiful and bright it
Makes the sun look black and flowers look ugly.
Your cheeks are redder than the reddest strawberry.
Your eyes are so golden and delightful
They make gold itself look cheap. Kiss me with the
Kisses of your lips. You are more precious than
Crystals and more worthy than gold. Your skin
Is smoother than silk. Compared to you Leonardo
Di Caprio is more wrinkly than an unironed shirt.

My love for you is stronger than iron and
Thicker than mud. You are Romeo and I am
Juliet. You are Sonny and I am Cher,
You are Antony and I am Cleopatra.
Must you torture me just because I am unloved?
Must you squash me like a beetle.
Your heart is blacker than coal. Your smell is worse
Than my sweat! Let me be. Tease me not.

(Inemesit, 12)

One boy wrote a riposte to his own excessive love speech ('Your hair hangs down like a blonde waterfall/Further down your body is a supermodel's body waiting/To be shown to the world') like this:

You cannot take me in by these false lies.
Why is it that you only love me now, and not then?
If you think I am so stupid to believe these lies
Then you can think again.

(Lee, 12)

Shakespeare the teacher has enabled Lee to see a female view of a certain element in maleness. His playing with Shakespeare is part of his work on moral education. For all children inspired by Shakespeare's lines, to write is to reflect on what it is to be a human being living in a society with all its resultant glories and confusions, with all the resultant moral difficulties and turbulence. At a healthy distance from the Prince's Bardic Swan of Avon, child- and adolescent-writers face the realities of the sexual nature. The riposte Lee had written for Helena took him no more than five minutes, and it is striking (to my ear at least) in its sincerity compared to his words for Demetrius. Lee's writing allowed at least one vivid metaphor (the waterfall) but, more importantly, allows him a go at rejecting the falsity of his writing with some lyrical vigour.

How did Inemesit arrange her lines? By luck (don't all teachers/writers/child-writers need luck?) I came across her just as she had finished writing 'Oh dear beloved, your hair is darker than the night sky' and I showed her how counting syllables might help her organize her speech, breaking the line like this: 'Oh dear beloved, your hair is darker/Than the night sky'. No-one would pretend this is going very far in the matter of prosody, or that her draft is thereby made up of iambic pentameters. But being aware of syllabic values is a beginning. This counting has fortuitously allowed Inemesit to begin lines effectively with 'Blood', 'Kisses', 'Crystal', 'Juliet' and 'Thicker'. This counting has also taught her something about the importance of verbs, as 'Makes' takes up a position more appropriate to the one it usually does.

Inemesit's poem ('Kiss me with the/Kisses of your lips') echoes the 'Song of Songs' in the Bible, where Chapter 1, verse 1 says 'Let him kiss me with the kisses of his mouth'. Although she is consciously writing insincere verse, the Shakespeare example has allowed Inemesit, like Sarah, to echo the cadences of traditional love poetry in different traditions, because, of course, Shakespeare's lines for Demetrius echo those cadences. Also 'unironed' subconsciously suggests 'iron' in the next line. The power of a word, its echo, stays in the writer's mind as she works. The phrase 'more worthy than gold' stands out because Inemesit seems to be using 'worthy' in its pristine sense.

Listening to Albert Finney's Romeo (1961) after I had taught these writers, I felt that their outrageously insincere love poems would prepare them for Romeo's expressions of his first love – for Rosaline, of course, not Juliet. It is intense – 'a smoke made with the fume of sighs…a sea nourished with loving tears…a madness most discreet,/A choking gall…'. It is also tiresome to his loving friend Benvolio, and, of course, it doesn't survive the first act. Children wrote poems based on these lines of Romeo's, and I print them on pp. 109–11.

Surely it won't always be night

Near the end of A Midsummer Night's Dream comes another passage that speaks to children. Puck is beginning to close things down, and he talks about the sounds of the night:

> Now the angry lion roars,
>   And the wolf behowls the moon,
> Whilst the heavy ploughman snores,
>   All with weary task foredone…
> Now it is the time of night
>   That the graves, all gaping wide,
> Every one lets forth his sprite
>   In the churchway paths to glide …
> I am sent with broom before
> To sweep the dust behind the door.
>
>   (V:1:361–80)

These are all extracts from poems written by nine-year-olds of a London school:

> Now it is the time of night
> I can hear
> the almost silent stream
> trickle over stones and pebbles…
> Now it is the time of night
> I can hear my hair
> scratching on my pillow.
> Now it is the time of night

Now I can hear my dreams…

(Lauren, 9)

That extract shows great aural sensitivity, especially in the words about the 'almost silent stream/[trickling] over stones and pebbles'. This child shows something that is learned during the junior years: an appropriate movement, in this case from the natural real world (the stream) to the emotional, almost the metaphysical (the dreams). Infants usually write, in contrast, a random collection of images. (See Charlotte's poem on p. 51).

Now it is the time of night
I can hear my fridge evaporate as I
snuggle deeper and deeper down into my bed
surely it won't always be night

(Danielle, 8)

This extract impressed me mostly for the little cry of help at the end: Danielle is one of those referred to by Edward Thomas in his penultimate poem 'Out in the Dark' (1981: 124–5):

How weak and little is the light,
All the universe of sight,
Love and delight,
Before the might,
If you love it not, of night.

Now it is the time of night
I can hear the stars singing above my head

(John, 9)

A turning point in the lesson had come when I told the children that the sounds did not have to be ones they could literally hear: they might be sounds they'd love to hear, and knew they never would. The next extract brought a touch of London social realism to the classroom, and a teacher commented afterwards, 'Well, Alex does live near to a pub'.

…Now it is the time of night
I hear people laughing outside my house
Now it is the time of night
I hear people throwing bottles when they're finished with them.
Now it is the time of night
I hear drunk people…

(Alex, 9)

Now it is the time of night
I hear my Dad snoring
and the wind and the rain talking to each other...

Now it is the time of night
The moon man is fishing for the sea...

(Jamie, 8)

That last line is a beautiful and (as far as I know) original description of the moon's effect on the tides. Again, it may have a grain of luck in it, but who cares? Like footballers, writers make their own luck.

Almost all these lines are from late in the poems. This is because, as in a PE lesson, children have to warm up. In the first ten minutes of the session, they composed conventional images, just as at the beginning of a PE session we are concerned with commonplace exercises involving stretching, jumping, turning and running. Two factors heightened the quality of the work: one was the practice they were getting in this warm-up, and the other was the plenary session we had after those ten minutes. Then, children read their work aloud and listened to other children. They then pollinated each other's writing by commenting on it. When each child who wanted to read out had done so, I commented on her writing, always positively, and encouraged other teachers present (and indeed, after a while the children) to do so too. I impressed on them that they were not to steal anyone's lines – but that they might be inspired by something someone else had written to write something fresh of their own. I called this activity 'editing friends'.

In another school, I did this exercise emphasizing the magic of the Shakespeare, and the results were quite different.

Now it is the time of night
when the ogres of anger
come out to the light
of purple fire which
burns in the sky of evil
and the fairies dance to
the music of the stars.
Now it is the time of night
when Zeus hurls bolts of lightning
down to the burning lava of ice from
the breech of a dragon's mouth
and the gods of Egypt attack the grizzling
goblins of the wood of blood.

Now it is the time of night when the tombs of
old kings blow up and their spirits crawl out
to cover the flowers of beauty.

Now it is the time of night when the werewolves of darkness
come out to the silver rays of the moon and fight, fight
in anger and kill each other.

Now it is the time of night when the
ghosts of evil attack the gnomes of heat
and kill many

   Now it is the time of night
to die in the flames of evil.

(Edward, 9)

In this poem, Edward seems to have found a release for much of his knowl-edge of games – computer games, possibly – and this release has led to a fluent, melodramatic reflection on evil. Other visions were happier: 'Now it is the time of night that/flames cha-cha round the gleaming bush…/the wind sings opera to the Hokey-cokey…/fairies conga round a stream of moonlight…'.

One group of children – half a village school aged from 7–9, plus two visitors from the nearby middle school, just there for the day because they wanted an opportunity to write – had written about Puck in many of the ways in which I have suggested. They'd written 'Follow you' poems, as I'd come to call them, and others based on this last idea. At the end of two intense days, I read the children riddles from Mole and Norman (1979), Crossley-Holland (1982) and Cotton and Sedgwick (1996). Here is an example of mine to give a flavour:

I am the emboldened sound
of the twentieth century.
Hear me in dim rooms
among smoke and glasses and heads that nod
just off the beat. Watch light
radiate like a child's star
from gold points on my horns
and know that oppression has made
my colours black and blue.
My satchel-mouthed saint
has played that thing,
gone marching in.

I asked the children to write riddles on themes and objects from *A Midsummer Night's Dream*. The answers to the riddle above, and to the following are on p. 150.

I live beneath hairy caterpillars
and hide when the sun does not shine
and sometimes when it does.

I have silk over me and under me
that flickers every three seconds.
My clothes come in different colours.
I exist on everyone
and my pupils have no teachers.

(Laura, 10)

I am clever
I am wicked, I am powerful and
magic. I creep around the forest and
jungles and I can run as fast as
a flash…

(Josh, 8)

I am a swirling creature,
First of all, I am invisible.
I am a magic vapour.
When I find something
I go all the colours of the world.
I make a quiet humming noise.
I make you feel damp and cold
and I leave dew drops in your hair.

(Helen, 9)

I am liquid kept in a bottle
or in a jar.
I should never be left in the wrong hands –
if I am something might go terribly wrong…

(Louisa, 11)

Chapter 3

A local habitation

The Tempest and *As You Like It*

The Tempest

Often children can gain much from some of the speeches that are considered of least consequence. In *The Tempest*, for example, while Prospero's 'I'll burn my books' presents problems, the shipwreck at the beginning of the play (I:1:1–60) is dramatic and not in the least obscure. As with 'I'll follow you', Shakespeare uses short phrases and lines to enact the commotion. For example:

> 'Mercy on us!' –
> 'We split, we split!' – 'Farewell, my wife and children!' –
> 'Farewell brother' –

I was with three teachers and over ninety children in a school hall, and I asked: Could the children imagine modern passengers and sailors drowning? Fortuitously, the film *Titanic* was in the news at the time, and some of the children had seen it. No doubt this helped. What might drowning passengers and sailors say? Very quickly the children compiled individual lists, from which the following are taken.

We're going down.

Life has gone so quickly.

Get the children in the boats or the water will swallow them in.

Save yourselves! I don't matter.

God save us please.

Why us?

God help the people back home

I want to go to heaven.

Help the ocean is swallowing us up.

The water's seeping through.

I shall miss the kids!

Well, guess this is it.

One neat error showed more writer's luck: 'What have we done to deserve depth?' Here the children are writing sentences that involve them in serious thinking about violent ends to lives, and at the same time they are examining a part of Shakespeare's dramatic method. To enrich the possibilities of both these activities, the children arranged themselves in pairs and acted their lines. Some only used the words, others brought actions into the session. Then pairs got together, and worked in fours, bawling out their lines alternately. One of the teachers showed the children how sometimes, even in a shipwreck, quiet, even inaudible things, like prayers, would be said: it wouldn't all be panicking bawling. Soon they had all written little plays with the title 'Shipwreck', and they performed them to each other around the hall. The session ended with a reprise of the lines from *The Tempest*, and the beginnings of the story of Prospero and Miranda.

Later in this play, Ariel sings the beautiful lament 'Full Fathom Five' that an inspector interrupted D H Lawrence teaching (see p. 4).

Full fathom five thy father lies,
Of his bones are coral made;
Those are pearls that were his eyes;
Nothing of him that doth fade,
But doth suffer a sea-change
Into something rich and strange.
Sea-nymphs hourly ring his knell.
Hark, now I hear them, ding dong bell.

(I:2:396–403)

I asked a group of children questions about these words, and their answers showed more flexibility and insight than, I think, most adults could show. The sea-change, for example, was not only the effect of the sea on the body, but also the change as the tide turns back. After reading the poem four or five times, with varying emphases and in different ways, I asked the children to imagine something they might have lost in the sea, and to write poems to mourn their losses. I pointed out to them the shape of 'Full fathom five', and the consistent length of its lines, which I merely counted in words.

At the bottom of the sea
Twenty miles down on the sea bed
There is a world globe sunk.
It's got a bit mouldy, rusty too.

The rust is thick and brown,
The mould is thick and green and furry.
A piece of it has been chipped off
And its stand has fallen off.

(Philip, 9)

The tinted Titanic sunk,
its hull down the bottom of the sea,
all its luggage going mouldy,
the silverware has lost its silver glow.
Human bones of the sufferers
are covered in seaweed.
Fish swim in and out of the ruins,
octopus, trout, salmon, in and out the Titanic.

(Natalie, 9)

We have to forgive a lack of knowledge of fish here! But for me at least it is easy to do so, because of the way this writer has used her viewing of the film *Titanic* to make such a simple elegy. The 'luggage' and the 'silverware' are telling details, neatly used. Also, this writer, like the other writers whose poems I have quoted, has picked up a hint I gave the children about the alliteration in Shakespeare's first line. All the writers have also picked up from the Shakespeare (and, it must be said, from my reading of his lines) an elegiac, mournful feel. They did not need these words explained: the poetry and my reading did the job for them. The poetry (pre-eminently) and my reading (in an infinitely minor way, compared to the poetry) are teachers themselves.

The witchful watch has been dropped,
it's getting ground away,
getting rusty as life goes on,
the silver going bronze,
the water breaking it to pieces,
eventually it looks like nothing,
it's sinking every minute,
down down down it goes.

(Christopher, 9)

Millions of miles down my Moggy lies.
His plastic eyes are pebbles now.
The string is the sea bed's blanket.
His velvet nose is coral now.
The time-taking stitching is seaweed now.
His metal build is flaky rust.

His velvet fur is torn by rocks…

(Amy-Jane, 9)

The last poem was written by a girl with evident difficulties in the mechanics of her writing. And yet these very difficulties have contributed to the odd magic of her poem: there is some domestic story mostly hidden in these peculiar lines, and the repetition is, if not exactly judged, got right by luck:

Ruby ruby ring ring round ring
went over with a ting ling
over went the ring screams from mother
she didn't seem to miss ring from papa
Ruby ruby ring ring round ring
lying on the bank green and rusty
golden shine gone now green green
Ruby ruby ring ring round ring

(Terry, 9)

Later in *The Tempest* Caliban has some of the most affecting lines from the plays, as he comforts Trinculo and Stephano who have been frightened (not, of course, that they'll admit it) by Ariel's music. I always feel here that there is something child-like in Caliban, Stephano and Trinculo as they come to terms with their 'local habitation', as there is with Bottom and the others as they prepare their play in *A Midsummer Night's Dream*.

Be not afeared, the isle is full of noises,
Sounds and sweet airs, that give delight, and hurt not.
Sometimes a thousand twangling instruments
Will hum about mine ears; and sometimes voices,
That if I then had waked after long sleep,
Will make me sleep again; and then in dreaming,
The clouds methought would open, and show riches
Ready to drop upon me, that when I waked
I cried to dream again.

(III:2:130–8)

Some of the poems had a romantic feel to them, like this one:

Be not afraid, the isle is full of noises…
Leaves crumble to the ground, making nothing but a single turn.
The wind whistles over the brick-made houses, twisting and turning around the hollow chimneys.
It sings silently beside the stained-glass windows of the newly-made houses.

The rain patterns past the wind and collides against the concrete ground
forming clear cold puddles of water

(Laura, 10)

Others were more practical in their attractions, like this next one, which reads
like a pornographic fantasy:

Be not afraid for the isle
is full of chocolates.
The brown sweet smell covers the island.
Brown shiny bumps on the land.
Chocolate leaves on the chocolatey
brown long thick trees.
The sun shines on the dark chocs
But magically the chocolate does not melt.

(Karan, 10)

...the isle is full of past and future visions
and you dance to the sweet Caribbean music...

(Iysha and Mushtaq, 10)

...The animals roam wild and free,
the horses without a harness or a bridle.
Light is shining on the great trees above
and the wind makes them rattle...
Gem stones hang silently on the willow
down by the crystal-clear water that shines like a mirror.

(Naomi, 10)

This is like the folk song 'Big Rock Candy Mountain', which is a childlike
vision of a perfect world ('O I'm bound to go where there ain't no snow,/Where
the rain don't fall and the wind don't blow'). Another related text is Isaiah's
vision of the holy mountain in Isaiah 11.

The wolf also shall dwell with the lamb, and the leopard shall lie down
with the kid; and the calf and the young lion and the fatling together; and
a little child shall lead them.

(verse 6)

These are words that Naomi, like other children, would love, and in another
session, when I've finished this book, I will do this again, using the Isaiah
passage and the American song alongside Caliban's words from *The Tempest*.

As You Like It

In the belief that children are concerned with issues that are conventionally called philosophical, I asked a group on a Pearse House course to write down some questions that 'they'd love to know the answer to, and yet knew they never would, at least this side of the grave' (see Sedgwick 1999 for a further account of this way of getting children thinking and writing, originally thought up as far as I can tell by Dawn Sedgwick). They wrote questions like:

> Is there life after death?
> Where did God come from?
> How old will I live to?
> Who invented the words we say?
> When the clock was invented how did they know the time?
> Why do we have to die?
> Is my life actually real?
> Do my friends all like me?
>
> (Abigail, 10)

One girl from a prep school wrote, memorably, 'Is Mrs —— having an affair with the Bursar?' I then read them Jaques's speech in II:7:12–34 of *As You Like It*. He has just come from talking with Touchstone, and the speech begins: 'A fool, a fool! I met a fool i' the forest,/A motley fool: a miserable world...' and climaxes with portentous truths: 'And so from hour to hour we ripe and ripe/And then from hour to hour we rot and rot...'.

I asked the children to write a passage beginning with the same line, but choosing another location; and ending with a reference, or even an answer to, the big questions they'd posed earlier.

> A fool, a fool! I met a fool in the park
> He wore jeans with great holes in
> and a baggy purple top.
> He was whistling and humming
> in a dreadful tune.
> When he whistled it sounded like
> a squeaky mouse being chased.
> He started speaking.
> It didn't make sense.
> I went up to him
> and I said.
> What a fool you are.
> He said This is the world
> and I live in it
> and he also told me how

the world spins
and how it orbits the sun.

(Thomas, 11)

A fool, A fool, I met a fool in the church.
She was wearing a scarf with a shabby dress.
For all I know I couldn't care less.
But the way she spoke to me it was
An evil voice all squeaky like nails on a blackboard.
She said things that I thought were rubbish.
Then out of the blue she told me why we die.
She explained it all in a strange sort of way.
You die so other people can see the world and live in it.
If you didn't die it wouldn't be fair.

(Anon, 11)

This last example shows a child-writer, inspired by Shakespeare's dramatic verse, exploring a question that she'd undoubtedly put to herself many times. 'You die so other people can see the world and live in it./If you didn't die it wouldn't be fair'. This is no more and no less than a hypothesis about the reason for death.

There are more questions in *As You Like It*. They seem to be a defining factor in Rosalind's character. Here, dressed, of course, as a man, she is desperate to know about her Orlando, whom Celia has just seen.

Alas the day, what shall I do with my doublet and hose? What did he have when thou saw'st him? What said he? How looked he? Wherein went he? What makes he here? Did he ask for me? Where remains he? How parted he with thee? And when shalt thou see him again? Answer me in one word.

(III:2:215–20)

I read this passage to a group of children, and then got them to learn one question each. We then put the questions to each other in different tones, having collected some adverbs first: angrily, worriedly, sadly, cheerfully, loudly, gently. At the end, we cried out in unison: 'Answer me in one word'. We said the speech again, with different groups saying different phrases. Soon, many of them had learned, quite painlessly, the whole speech. I then put the children in various imaginary situations, such as being about to receive a present, being told they are about to change schools, and about to go on holiday to a place 'where no-one has ever been before'. I asked the children to make a prose speech of questions.

Is it an exotic place? Will it be a dangerous expedition? Why do we have to go there? Which hotel will we be staying at? How long is the journey going to take? When are we going to go? Will it surrounded by water? Will I never want to come back once I get there? Am I having to go by car, boat or aeroplane? Is it cold or it is hot at the amazing place? Will I hear noises that no-one has ever heard before? What sort of things will I see? Will I go on adventures? Will I hear the wind blowing in my face? Tell me the answers quicker than a streak of lightning.

(Kavita, 8)

This speech starts dully as the writer begins to warm up; by the ending she is writing with feeling. This was true of many of the pieces, as it has been of many of the pieces throughout this book. These are the final lines of one:

Do the flowers sing? Do the waves crash against the rocks? Will the grass sway from side to side? Tell me, tell me, in the sway of a tree.

(Hannah, 8)

And these are the final lines of another:

Can I listen and see the colours of the wind? Can I eat fresh coconuts? Answer me like wind!

(Anon, 8)

The children were asked to think of a clinching final line, like Rosalind's. Offers included 'Answer me in a sizzling sentence', 'Answer me in a flash of wind' and 'Give me my answer before I scream'.

Other children wrote questions they would ask if they had been told a boy or girl 'wanted to go out with them':

Is he nice? Will we see Titanic together or apart? Does he ride a motorbike? Will his hair glide like the wind? Is he sweet? Is his hair purple? Is he dumb? Will he murder me? Will his ear-ring glitter in the sunshine? Are his teeth yellow? Does he wear anything cool? Does he smell of aftershave?

(Jenny, 9)

There were differences between the boys' and the girls' ideas. The boys' writing about presents tended to be more materialistic than the girls'. Also, the boys writing about meeting girls was sexist: 'Will she be off Baywatch? Will she be hot? Does she cook well?'; though one boy asked 'Has she got flowing hair like a stream? Is she beautiful inside?' The girls, on the other hand, were neither sexist nor materialistic. The exercise led me to much the same provisional conclusions as an earlier experiment. I had asked children to write kennings about the opposite sex, and to write poems composed of thoughts as a man or a woman does household jobs (see Sedgwick 1994: Chapter 5). Both these experiments led me to much the same conclusion: that boys still inherit the sexist values of the generations before them.

The last example from *As You Like It* was the first writing I did for this book.

Fourteen children, ranging in age from 8–11 and working in pairs listened to the famous 'Seven Ages of Man' speech in *As You Like It*.

> All the world's a stage,
> And all the men and women merely players.
> They have their exits and their entrances;
> And one man in his time plays many parts,
> His acts being ages seven. At first the infant,
> Mewling and puking in the nurse's arms;
> Then the whining schoolboy, with his satchel
> And shining morning face, creeping like snail
> Unwillingly to school. And then the lover,
> Sighing like furnace, with a woeful ballad
> Made to his mistress' eyebrow. Then a soldier,
> Full of strange oaths, and bearded like the pard
> …
>
> And then the justice,
> In fair round belly with good capon lin'd,
> With eyes severe and beard of formal cut…
> The sixth age shifts
> Into the lean and slippered pantaloon,
> With spectacles on nose and pouch on side,
> His youthful hose, well sav'd, a world too wide
> For his shrunk shank; and his big manly voice,
> Turning again towards childish treble, pipes
> And whistles in his sound. Last scene of all,
> That ends this strange eventful history,
> Is second childishness and mere oblivion;
> Sans teeth, sans eyes, sans taste, sans everything.
>
> (II:7:139–66)

I explained some difficult terms, such as 'pard', 'woeful ballad/Made to his mistress' eyebrow', and 'sans', and asked the children to write their own version:

> We live on a film set and we are the actors.
> We come and go
> And we have seven different parts.
> First the infant
> Crying for his bottle full of milk,
> Going to the toilet in his fourth pair of pull-ups today,
> Playing with his brand new toy,
> Mother saying 'Clever boy!'
> Next Jane the schoolgirl –

Brown sandals, white socks pulled up to her knees
Wanting to wear her plimsolls and have her socks down,
Leather satchel with one sandwich in a box
Wanting two. She'd rather be at home
Playing with her china dollies.
Then the boy thinking about
The snog he received last night
And a good future of infants
And a bad future of changing smelly nappies.
Fourth, a three-stripes helping the law with doubts,
Moustachioed, dark eyebrows to match.
And then the school governor
Growing plump with the addition of
Grey hairs and a furry chin.
Sixth is Grandpa who reaches out
For his old grey pipe
With his haggard shaking hand;
Stretching out for his false teeth
Sterilising in the jam jar.
Last a baby again with wrinkly old face
And a tuft of white hair. Needs a new battery
In his hearing aid. Won't go out anymore.
Disintegrating. Shrinking away.

This poem was odd for me because of idioms I didn't know: 'pull-ups' and 'three-stripes'. More to the point, it included girls, as Shakespeare's lines don't; and it faded away appropriately. In another school, children wrote individual poems for each age:

Schoolboy:

That schoolboy scuffing his shoes
as he drags them behind!
That schoolboy squirming his way into school!
That schoolboy slouching over his work!
That schoolboy day-dreaming the time away!
That schoolboy running to home in joyful glee!
That schoolboy slouching across the couch!

(John and Michael, 9)

The writers of that poem have clearly taken on the power of Shakespeare's verbs: compare his 'creeping' to their 'scuffing', 'slouching' and 'squirming'. Indeed, other words in the original ('mewling' and 'puking', for example) have had their effect on these boys. Also, an unusual thing has happened: the hyperbolic use of the exclamation mark is appropriate here. The boys seem to be reflecting wryly on their own memories and current lives. Here is another schoolboy, seen from a girl's point of view: he

> slithers clumsily along the footpath
> gazing grumpily at the ground
> turning into the school gates creeping like a spider...
>
> (Emma, 10)

Here is a frightening schoolgirl:

> Groaning, moaning schoolgirl
> walking like a tortoise
> slouching all the way
> muttering to herself.
> She is thin as a rake
> and a vicious as a fox.
> Teacher does not think much of her.
>
> (Sarah Jane, 9)

And a soldier, followed by a judge:

> Then a soldier full of strength and bravery
> Ready for action
> and as sudden as a bullet
> Seeking an ambush with his fellow mates –
> He never gives up hope.
> The judge gracefully glides along
> With an air of elegance about her
> She walks pompous past in her royal red robes
> The standing people with their hearts running riot respect her for
>   all that she is.
>
> (John)

When I was working with these children, I made no reference to issues like line length, iambic pentameters or syllabic counts. Thus the poems are written in organic length lines. Later I discovered that there were ways of making the poems resemble the originals at least in appearance and sometimes in sound by getting the children to look at the appearance of the lines. These two writers working together carefully counted syllables.

> That old toothless man sipping soup slowly
> And the spoon going into that dark mouth.
> He has no taste as he sips that pea soup

And his gums burn as he spits out the last drop.

Finally, an over-the-top (I hope) but very vivid image of an old man:

> My Grandad has
> wrinkled skin and yellow
> teeth crippled back and walking
> stick cut out sack to make a hat
> buckled shoes and a bald head
> too skinny legs croaky voice ragged
> clothes and a dribbly nose thats
> my Grandad Jones.
>
> (Pamara, 10)

By making versions of Jaques' speech, children study the original more effectively than they would if they were merely reading it. More effectively, too, than if they were reading it to write a critical essay about it and, arguably, more effectively than if they were studying the speech to learn it for acting purposes. I do not say that there is no time and no place for casual reading, writing critical essays and rote learning. But in having to translate Shakespeare's words into their own, children take ownership of Shakespeare's words as well as their own, and his words will, in all likelihood, never let them go. And those words will not solidify in their brains. They will ferment and reproduce, changing meanings as years go by. Their effects will grow with further learning. They will come to relevances that are now invisible, unimaginable, to those children.

Sandy Brownjohn (1989: Chapter 18) has an account of children writing using this speech. She says:

> I asked the class to think of writing something themselves…about anything mentioned in the speech or [they could] use an idea sparked off by something they had read…they could use a line or phrase from the text to use as a title or basis from which to write…

The children in her class produced vivid writing; the grandfather, for example, 'reading the newspaper./His voice crumbles away as he speaks'. Brownjohn goes on to say that the children were 'inspired to greater heights than usual' because of 'the presence of the Master':

> …if the examples put in front of [children] are the best…[they] will aim higher and raise their standards.…I intend to use other famous speeches as stimuli for writing…

I don't know if she has done that. The writing in her book and, I believe, in mine, proves her first sentence true.

Interval

Thou drone, thou snail, thou slug, thou sot

I have already said in my Introduction how important it is for children to be introduced to the work of Shakespeare without the sentimental accretions that stick on it because of the way the Prince of Wales and others talk about it, and the way storytellers emasculate it. The first time I saw an excellent (and indeed, I think, innovative) book on this subject, *Shakespeare's Insults* by Wayne F Hill and Cynthia J Ottchen: 1991) I realized that the tendency of Shakespeare's characters towards habits of abuse of extreme kinds would come in handy in the relatively sedate atmosphere of most primary school classrooms. A wonderfully vigorous seam of insult, of ridicule, of rudeness, or derision, of scurrility, of mocking crackles electrically throughout the plays. In his indispensable study of swearing, foul language, oaths and profanity, Hughes (1998) writes of 'a great chorus of curses' in the history plays

> which reaches its climax in *Richard III* with the virulent invective of Margaret. Shunning the run-of-the-mill insults such as dog, cur and devil, she employs a spectacular gamut of vituperation...

and Hughes quotes:

> Thou slave of nature and the son of hell!
> Thou slander of thy mother's heavy womb!
> Thou loathed issue of thy father's loins!
>
> (I:3:230–2)

Other less appalling insults provide an invaluable way into Shakespeare's work for children under eleven years, and enable us as teachers to emphasize characters like Falstaff and his friends in the Henry plays, the Porter in *Macbeth*, Sir Toby Belch in *Twelfth Night*, Trinculo and Stephano in *The Tempest*, and the ruffians rather than the royals in *A Midsummer Night's Dream*. Hill and Ottchen's book supplies us with a memorable collection of insults, and, in doing so, stops us making Shakespeare an elegant figure to be celebrated for the sweetness of his tongue. Rather, it shows him up as something far more vital: a celebrator of life and death in all its forms, and throbbing with the beat of the most common, the most vulgar, speech. These characters' insults still have the power to chill us, if we listen: 'A pox o' your throat, you bawling, blasphemous, incharitable dog! You whoreson, insolent noisemaker…' At the end of *King Lear*, the insults are terrifying.

'People *need* insults' Hill and Ottchen tell us. 'Most people behave so abominably that they cry out for abuse. Charity moves us to meet this need'. Children suggest that Hill and Ottchen are right, because I have found that children write insults with an exuberant and creative glee. First, this is for a reason I have noted before: the word 'wicked' had a double meaning among children until recently. Insulting each other came into this category, but of course they felt protected from each other's excesses by the fact that the insults were, as they saw it, 'only lines from poems'. One teacher noted later how valuable the exercise was because it gave the children the chance to abuse each other without swearing. Second, children need to abuse as much as adults, and the classroom is the best place in which to learn how to do it with anything like a touch of class.

This first poem was written on a Pearse House course. On the second day, I felt ready to insult the children with some words picked at random from Hill and Ottchen:

> You stony image, cold and dumb; thou map of woe; base bondsman; joyless, dismal and sorrowful issue; hellish dog; sanguine, shallow-hearted boy; ye white-limed wall; ye alehouse painted sign; long-tongued babbling gossip; sly frantic wretch; incarnate devil; execrable wretch…

This caused much merriment, especially on the part of the child being insulted. I then told the children that I knew about the solar system (as that knowledge was in 1958, when I did a topic on it at grammar school: Neptune and Uranus didn't have rings then). I warned them that I would now insult someone in terms of that knowledge. They clamoured for the honoured place next to me, and I said to someone:

> You are so cold Neptune would suit me better for a holiday than you.
> You wandering asteroid,
> You are a red spot on the face of a dead planet
> and your brain is as thin as Saturn's rings.
> I wish I was as far from you
> as Pluto is from Mercury.
> I wish I could hear your voice
> as loud as I can hear Mars spinning.
> I wish you were hidden from me
> by a misty veil like the one round Venus…

and so on. Then I used my knowledge of jazz. Miri used food to write her poem. Given that she is Jewish, her first line is all the more powerful:

You half-eaten pork pie
you could make a dragon cry.
You look like
sicked-up minced beef
or a chewed-up caterpillar on a leaf.
You are a waffle all squashed
or mashed-up peas...

(Miri, 10)

Another writer used her knowledge of music:

You're so small
you make a piccolo look colossal.
Even a breve can go faster than you.
You look like a piano that hasn't been used for 200 years.
You make noises like a wrongly-blown trumpet.
Even Beethoven had a better hair-style than you.
A euphonium has a smaller bell than your mouth...

(Rajiv, 11)

Later, I asked another group of children to arrange their insults into haiku form (three lines: five, seven and five syllables in each). This meant that they had to think further about structure, and about whether each word was doing sufficient work:

You broken record
you're so out of pitch you break
glass windows. You are

a tone deaf flute. You
sound like fingernails down a
very old blackboard.

You're a broken drum,
a snapped in half recorder.
You sing like thunder.

Mice can sing better
than you. A yowling cat can
mew better than you.

(Faye, 11)

After a while, I felt it would be more truthful to Shakespeare's spirit to concentrate on one character in a session, and his sustained insults. I chose Prince Hal in *Henry IV Part 1*. Falstaff has just asked him for 'the time of day' and the Prince responds with contemptuous vigour:

> Thou art so fat-witted with drinking of old sack, and unbuttoning thee after supper, and sleeping upon benches after noon, that thou hast forgotten to demand that truly which thou woulds't truly know. What a devil hast thou to do with the time of the day? Unless hours were cups of sack, and minutes capons, and clocks the tongues of bawds, and dials the sound of leaping houses, and the blessed sun himself a fair hot wench in flame-coloured taffeta...

> (I:2)

The question of propriety that I broached in my Introduction arose here, and at this point I will simply confess to cowardice: I left out the bawds, the leaping houses and the 'fair hot wench in flame-coloured taffeta'. I remembered this last lady vividly and with affection from my study of the play at O-level, and regretted betraying her here with these children. ('You prude, Fred!' says my friend Mary Jane Drummond, woundingly.) Of course, the problem here is our embarrassment, not the children's potential corruption: no child is going to be made sexually incontinent by these bawds. We are simply protecting ourselves. How much of our teaching is similarly compromised? I then asked the children to decide whom they would like to insult. The first writer chose a bully:

> What time is it?
> Why do you want to know
> you who are such a big fat bully
>
> why don't you roll yourself to the nearest clock...
>
> If hours was kids and minutes geeks and seconds was doops you
> would find the time much quicker than me to tell you...
>
> (Alex, 10)

'Geeks' and 'doops' are, as I write, current words for the easily bullied. 'Geeks' appear again in the next section. Current slang seems to be appropriate here, given Shakespeare's use of his contemporary slang, much as the ungrammatical use of 'was' for 'were' seems to be right for the speech. 'Why don't you roll yourself to the nearest clock' has the right mix of appropriateness and the will to wound. I enjoyed this writing for its obscurity: why should not children's writing, like nearly all creative writing, occasionally have references that are not open to every reader? Another example is in my 1997 book, where Eloise, a passionate Liverpool fan, writes about her father: 'I run through the tunnel and touch you for luck'. Few readers will know that the team touch the club crest above their heads on the mouth of the tunnel as they run out to play at home. The infant writing about the 'harowing raptors' had written words that only he, I suspect, can understand.

One writer's insults achieved a direct fluency as she attacked a miser:

> ...You only have your money to comfort you. Even the ugliest girl would turn you down, for a woman would rather stick a knife in her heart than marry a mean tight-fisted penny-pinching miser like you...
>
> (Sharon, 10)

In *All's Well That End's Well*, Lord Lafew insults the cowardly Parolles more or less continuously for nearly fifty lines of prose, calling him a 'hen', a 'vagabond', and 'Sirrah' – a word used only for servants and children. He belittles his status, wishes him in hell, abuses his manner of dress, threatens him and tells him coarsely where he should put his manhood. In their edition of this play, Huddlestone and Innes suggest a useful insult game: 'Identify all the insults Lafew uses to Parolles....Stand in a circle with one person as Parolles in the centre and shout the insults at him. Take turns at being in the centre'. They comment: 'It is an unpleasant experience' and ask 'How can you make it comical?' Though their main aim here is to help secondary pupils to understand the play better, and possibly act in it, this technique would lead to vivid writing with our primary school writers.

One way of giving the insult poem a sharper focus is to read the children Petruchio's denunciation of the tailor who has made his wife's dress in *The Taming of the Shrew*.

> Thou liest, thou thread, thou thimble,
> Thou yard, three-quarters, half-yard, quarter, nail,
> Thou flea, thou nit, thou winter-cricket thou!
> ...
> Away, thou rag, thou quantity, thou remnant,
> Or I shall so be-mete thee with thy yard
> As thou shalt think on prating while thou livest...
>
> (IV:3:107–14)

I pointed out to a group of children how these lines have used words from the tailor's trade: 'thread', 'thimble', 'yard', etc. and asked them to write insults for particular professions. Near the school where this poem was written, town planners had set up sixteen traffic lights on a medium-sized roundabout, and had thereby provoked a minor *cause célèbre* in the area and in the local press. One girl felt very strongly about this, and her poem shows this, in spite of (or perhaps in part because of) its inarticulacy:

You slowed down stupid hags from the council
stopped the flow you big fat weasels
you have no use with you
old squashed up sandbags
You are sun black old cabbages on everyone's feet
You red yellow and banged up to right lights
you old dirt of somebody's worries.

(Sophie, 8)

Another child insulted a greengrocer:

You mouldy old Discovery apple
Away with you and your cabbage
Your turnip and cucumber
Away with you decrepit old sack
Which you carry your black and brown potatoes in
Your brown paper which always splits…

(Sophie, 9)

One boy wrote to a doctor 'away with your stupid old piles', meaning pills, but I think now that the teacher and I had sound instincts when we persuaded him to leave the line as he had fortuitously written it.

An assortment of insults culled mostly from plays not otherwise used in this book

All's Well That Ends Well

In his sleep he does little harm, save to the bedclothes around him
(IV:3:246–8)

This is wonderfully foul and subtle, suggesting more about bodily secretions than I care to type up. I feel sure that children could echo this line, when asked to replace 'sleep' and 'bedclothes' with other words. 'In his garden he does no wrong, except to the wall when he leans on it' is one suggestion. Children will do better.

The Comedy of Errors

The easiest kind of insulting is in this play: this is the simple list which makes its effect cumulatively:

Thou drone, thou snail, thou slug, thou sot

(II:2:194)

Mome, malthouse, capon, coxcomb, idiot, patch!
(mome = blockhead)

(III:1:32)

Rahima used the playground for a list of insults:

...Stone, hard ground, broken climbing frame!
Bully's thoughts, stupid person's brain
boring game of chase, a big miss at rounders...

(Rahima, 6)

And Neill used the painting table:

Empty paintpot, flicky bit of dried paint, old hairless brush, torn paper...

(Neill, 7)

Coriolanus

He that trusts to you,
Where he should find you lions, finds you hares;
Where foxes, geese. You are no surer, no,
Than is the coal of fire upon the ice,
Or hailstone in the sun.

(I:1:169–73)

Children write following this example, again, to satirize the person who
promises more than he or she gives:

If I followed you, mate,
I'd find you'd lost me in the crowd...

(Bethany, 12)

Henry IV Part 2

I scorn you, scurvy companion. What, you poor, base, rascally, cheating,
lack-linen mate! Away, you mouldy rogue, away!

Another useful list.

Julius Caesar

> – He is a tried and valiant soldier.
> – So is my horse.

(IV:1:28–9)

This provides a possibility for a deflating insult after faint praise. I gave children the first lines here, and they followed up with the insults:

> – He is a clever boy.
> – At rudeness, fidgeting and kicking under tables.

(Simon, 9)

> – She is good at games.
> – Yes, kiss-chase.

(Marian, 12)

> – She runs well.
> – Backwards!

(John, 9)

Others were pleasingly bizarre:

> – She's a great pet settler.
> – If you like dead pets.

(Jack, 7)

> – She can calculate huge numbers.
> – So can my calculator.

(Amy, 10)

> – He's got such a pretty neck.
> – Shame it's got bolts in it.

(Billie, 9)

> – She's a good singer.
> – If you like broken glass.

(Matthew, 9)

> – He's a brilliant woodcutter.
> – So is my beaver.

(Thomas, 8)

Titus Andronicus

> Foul-spoken coward, that thund'rest with thy tongue,
> And with thy weapon nothing dar'st perform!
>
> (II:1:58–9)

Children happily write insults about people who promise more than they achieve:

> Loud-mouth striker that goes on all week
> about your goals on Saturday, and scores none!
>
> (Eleanor, 12)

* * *

Gibson (1988) has a splendid technique for making children familiar with the vigour of Shakespeare's insults and curses. It is based on a play we have already looked at, *The Tempest*: 'List and number an equal number of Prospero–Caliban exchanges...' Gibson suggests, offering the following examples from I:2: 321–64:

CALIBAN: As wicked dew as e'er my mother brushed
With raven's feather from unwholsome fen
Drop on you both.
A south-west blow on ye
And blister you all o'er.

All the charms
Of Sycorax – toads, beetles, bats light on you!

You taught me language, and my profit on't
Is, I know how to curse. The red plague rid you
For learning me your language!

PROSPERO: For this, be sure, tonight thou shalt have cramps,
Side-stitches that shall pen thy breath up.
Urchins
Shall for that vast of night that they may work
All exercise on thee.
  Thou shalt be pinched
As thick as honey-comb, each pinch more stinging
Than bees that made 'em.

I'll rack thee with old cramps,

> Fill all thy bones with aches, make thee roar,
> That beasts shall tremble at thy din…

Then, Gibson suggests, 'students stroll (lovely word in this context, contrasting as it does with the words being spoken) around the room greeting each other with one or two curses…' This sounds perfect! In the terms of this book, they could then go to the quiet of a desk, and write further curses and insults in the style of Caliban's and Prospero's.

Another kind of insult is the flattering speech which attempts to disguise the speaker's real feelings, and which changes their meaning to the opposite. *Richard II* I:1:20–4 offers an example. Bolingbroke and Mowbray vie with each other to impress the King with honeyed words:

BOLINGBROKE: Many years of happy life befall
>   My gracious sovereign, my most loving liege!
MOWBRAY: Each day still better other's happiness,
>   Until the heavens…
>   Add an immortal title to your crown!

There is more on flattery at p. 117 (in *King Lear*).

Why Petruchio is coming

Finally in this interlude, before we return to the main agenda and enter the darkness of one of Shakespeare's tragedies, we look at two moments from *The Taming of the Shrew*. This, like *The Merchant of Venice*, is one of Shakespeare's troubling plays, because its subject is the subduing of a woman. What makes it worse to modern ears is that at the end, the woman, Katherina, accepts her subjugation, and recommends it to other women. It is difficult, reading this play, to see how it can be performed today without great irony or bitterness: Petruchio, the 'hero', is a bullying misogynist of the worst kind.

In the first scene, the servant Biondello announces the arrival of Petruchio at his own wedding. This is not really to do with insults, but the passage is a rich description of carelessness at would-be grandeur and it fits here. There are probably more obscure words in this short passage than there are in any comparable passage in the complete works. They are not abstract words; they are completely specific and concrete; and contrary to popular belief, children enjoy such words, whether they know the meanings or not. They are great fun and should be read, listened to and, above all, tasted. And the structure of the passage is simply a list. As Gill (1996) says, this speech must be spoken very quickly. As it is relatively unfamiliar, I give it all here.

> Why, Petruchio is coming in a new hat and an old jerkin; a pair of old
> breeches thrice turned; a pair of boots that have been candle-cases, one

buckled, another laced; an old rusty sword ta'en out of the town armoury, with a broken hilt, and chapeless; with two broken points; his horse hipped, with an old mothy saddle and stirrups of no kindred; besides, possessed with the glanders, and like to mose in the chine, troubled with the lampass, infected with the fashions, full of windgalls, sped with spavins, rayed with the yellows, past cure of the fives, stark spoiled with the spives, begnawn with the bots, swayed in the back and shoulder-shotton, near-legged before, and with a half-cheeked bit and a headstall of sheep's leather which, being restrained to keep him from stumbling, hath been often burst, and new-repaired with knots; one girth six times pieces, and a woman's crupper of velour, which hath two letters for her name fairly set down in studs, and here and there pieced with pack-thread.

(III:2:41–60)

I practised this at home several times till I could say it very fast. I got a group of ten and eleven-year-olds to say the words after me. ('glanders, glanders…lampass, lampass…windgalls, windgalls…spavins, spavins…') I told them what most of the words meant, though we guessed some. I noticed how much they enjoyed the sound of them; that their obscurity did not matter to them. There is a selective glossary for this speech, derived from Gill, in the Appendix (page 150). I then asked the children to imagine an eccentric man or woman arriving inappropriately dressed for his or her wedding. I suggested that they loaded the speech with vivid, focused and accurate words. As their characters probably wouldn't come on a horse, I suggested they describe the car they arrived in.

Bernard is coming in worn-out brown sandals, probably not even good quality leather. He is wearing polyester and nylon blue trousers, baggy, but too tight around his ankles. His socks have several holes and they are geeky woollen red and blue stripes, clashing horribly with his patchy old trousers and sandals. Then, to make that worse, he wears a mauve sleeveless collared shirt with tatty, badly-made frills along the edge of the shoulder. He wears a hat which is yellow with a pink rose attached. He arrives in a smashed-up Mini that looks like someone has used it on a scrambling track (they probably did before he bought it for £15) It is light pink with rusty and dirty parts and the seats are light brown moth-eaten material. The tyres are flat and have never been changed. When they get a hole he patches it up with tape. The floor has oil stains, mustard stains, ketchup stains and blood stains. The number plate is G252EEK. When he brakes there is an ear-piercing screech even though his highest speed is 35 m.p.h.

(Lizbeth, 11)

This piece shows an attention to the Biondello speech (compare 'not even good quality leather' with 'a headstall of sheep's leather'), an awareness of 'good' and 'bad' in clothes ('polyester and nylon blue trousers'), a neat use of modern slang ('geeky') and an expert's knowledge of what doesn't match in colour. It took about fifteen minutes to write, and it enabled Lizbeth to practise her fluency.

The Bridegroom has arrived!

He's dressed in his work clothes which are all greasy with oil. His footwear are trainers all covered with holes. His shirt is soaking from a bus which has run through a puddle and squirted him. His jeans are grubby with stained of baked beans…no tie, no suit, he is a total wreck!…

(Daniel, 11)

Other children described different personalities arriving at their weddings, and they all demonstrated a delight with words and a sense of comedy. There were teachers, a vicar, pop stars and politicians:

He arrives at last. He climbs out of his car talking, and no-one else can get a word in edgeways. Even on his wedding day, he goes on and on and on about policy and committees, and ministries, and chairmen and office and portfolios, of administration. He talks about briefs and steering groups and parties…

(Callum, 12)

I suspect this piece owed something to a thesaurus.

Eventually, as we study Shakespeare, we have to go beyond the slapstick of *The Comedy of Errors*, beyond the dark resolved mysteries of *A Midsummer Night's Dream*, beyond the impenetrable knowledge of *The Tempest*, beyond the need for abuse as we move through the world peopled by fools, including, above all, ourselves. We have to tread warily into a night where the magic is never benevolent, and always truthful; where the foolishness is sometimes the foolishness of a silly man or woman like Bottom and his friends, but often, in contrast, is the foolishness of wild ambition; of some terrible obsession that will leave the play ending in the inevitable way that the Greek tragedies ended: with a stage littered with bodies.

Chapter 4

How goes the night, boy?

Macbeth

Shakespeare's tragedies obviously present problems for the primary school teacher. The moral complexity of *Hamlet* and *King Lear*, and the latter's theme of learning through age and madness, as well as its violence, and Lear's 'terror at female sexuality' (Hughes 1992), make both these plays problematic (though Gilmour 1997: Chapter 7 has an interesting account of children working with *King Lear*). The sexual jealousy and treachery in *Othello* is largely beyond children, and they have not yet reached even the beginning of the 'salad days' that Cleopatra, in her incipiently decadent ripeness, so sardonically dismisses. *Julius Caesar* and *Coriolanus* are highly political plays. All these works pre-suppose experiences most children simply have not had.

Two tragedies, though, have plenty to say to children. *Romeo and Juliet's* themes – 'love and hate, fate and free will, life and death, youth against age,…luck' (Gibson 1998:20) – are magnetic ones for young people. The problem with this play is not inherent in Shakespeare's text, but in the fact that, if present trends continue, it is the only play that large numbers of a generation of children will know, because of its prominence in the national curriculum. I include some work from this play later.

The other tragedy that works on the minds of children when they play with it is *Macbeth*, which is less hackneyed by our politicians and their hired hands. Where does the power of this play for young writers lie? First, Hell is present on the edge of nearly every scene in *Macbeth*, and in the centre of some scenes, and many children are worried about the existence of Hell. You don't have to be Stephen Dedalus, schooled by Christian brothers, or Billy Connolly, with A-levels in guilt, to wonder about what happens if you've been unkind to your brothers and sisters or disrespectful to the headteacher or the priest, or 'been unclean in your habits' (thus have I heard one ex-prep schoolboy talk) after death. I have already quoted one child writing 'surely it won't always be night' in my discussion of Puck's speech near the end of *A Midsummer Night's Dream*. She may well spend some of each night in fear of what should happen if she died. We are not so far from the times when children sang in Sunday schools and elsewhere 'And if I die before I wake/I pray the Lord my soul to take'.

Children think about Hell in another, deeper way: they know about the Hell that it can be to live human life, working and playing, laughing and crying with other people. The conflicts on the playground may look trivial to adult eyes, but they are not so trivial to the children involved in them. From close up, they have the scale of battles. And many children face the Hell of other people in grimmer ways than that, as we can read in newspapers every day of the week. *Macbeth* is about all this kind of experience, and children recognize it in the play. Ruston (1998) tells a disturbing story that suggests, however, that the Hell we live in is sometimes too much for us and the art we choose:

> I was studying *Macbeth* with a GCSE group when the Dunblane massacre occurred. Suddenly, in the middle of a lesson we all felt that *Macbeth* was just too repulsive at that moment because we all felt too shaken by events.

Second, children are also concerned with their consciences, and *Macbeth* is about conscience. Later, I offer revealing examples of children responding to Lady Macbeth's words in the sleepwalking scene. The play is also about (as Gilmour 1997: Chapter 10 says) 'friendship and loyalty', and it offers opportunities to 'explore issues such as making friends and falling out, and facing up to the moral dilemma of when to tell on your friends and when not'. And, of course, many children like the bloodshed: 'Personally I like a lot of blood and guts in a film, and I can recommend this for anyone a bit like me' a ten-year-old says in Gilmour. We have all learned by now what this writer calls 'the lesson of *Lord of the Flies*' and do not sentimentally believe in the innocence of childhood. *Macbeth* offers us the chance to explore with children violence and its justification at certain times; state, official violence as opposed to what would be thought of as criminal violence; even the psychological violence we do to ourselves and each other. The Porter's speech, of which much more later, offers children a rare opportunity to do violence in words: to be satirists.

A simpler reason for studying *Macbeth* is that it is an exciting, elemental play, and it is very fast: Macbeth arrives home, and there is no sentiment to speak of in his first conversation with his wife. Indeed, within a few lines they've discussed the death of Duncan. After the bawdy speech of the Porter there is, almost immediately, the discovery of the murder. It is a short play, full of hellish happenings tumbling on top of one another; it's full of alarum-bells, murder and treason. And at least one of its images – the witch – is part of most children's myth-kitty before they come to school, because, often, they know stories by the Brothers Grimm, Hans Christian Andersen and others, and because they are familiar with Disney through television, film and video. Also, the witches speak in largely accessible language.

They present, however, problems: there is talk among evangelical Christians which suggests that witches should not be talked about, written about or in any other way depicted to young children. I have even been asked not to read poems about Hallowe'en in schools. I don't want to waste too many words on this notion. More to the point, we have to make sure that we do not stereotype the witches as wicked old women. There is much scope here for fresh interpretations of the scenes in where they appear: are they emanations from Macbeth's mind? Why, notwithstanding their evident depravity, can they not be young, attractive people of either sex? (They would, of course, in Shakespeare's day, have been played by men.) And we should remember too that they prophesy, and get things right: they must be more than mad hags.

Macbeth has, as Hughes (1992) writes, 'come to feel like the most essential expression of Shakespeare's tragic and poetic vision'. If this play is less sexual than *Hamlet*, *Othello* and the others (the ever-alert Partridge (1948: 46) tells us that it 'is the "purest" of the Tragedies and, except for the Porter scene, pure by any criterion') this is because the lust in the play is lust for power. Hughes convincingly suggests that Macbeth is like Tarquin in 'The Rape of Lucrece' throughout the play: not only as he creeps through the palace to murder Duncan. Indeed, Macbeth recognizes this himself: he walks 'with Tarquin's ravishing strides' (II:1:55). This lack of normal sexuality may seem like good news because it is therefore less problematic to teach. But in fact, *Macbeth* is, in places, disturbingly anti-sexual, anti-love, anti-family. Lady Macbeth famously prays 'Unsex me here'.

She is more interested in the aphrodisiac of power than in her husband and her babies who never appear, but who are present in frightening lines: 'I...know/How tender 'tis to love the babe that milks me;/I would while it was smiling in my face/Have plucked the nipple from his boneless gums/And dashed the brains out, had I so sworn as you/Have done to this' (I:7:54–9). The Porter takes another angle on sex when he talks about the way drink can both incite lechery and discourage it. The sexual references in all of Shakespeare's plays may present teachers with problems of several kinds. When they are present in *Macbeth* then they are less 'reechy' and 'wanton' to use Hamlet's terrible words to his mother, and more disgusted.

The tyranny of the whole play

For these and other reasons, I have had no difficulty in finding vivid work by children based on this play, and in developing writing ideas from it myself. But first I must write a note about an issue that arises naturally here. There is an unnecessary tyranny that adds to the intimidation factor in much teaching of Shakespeare. This is the tyranny of the whole play. I watched an English advisory teacher introduce, in assembly, a junior school to *Macbeth* by spending fifty minutes telling the complete story, and not, as far as I could tell, missing out one single detail ('...And then this captain, who had blood all over his face, said...'). There was even a paraphrase (though, of course, bowdlerized) of the Porter's speech. All this was done with formidable energy and evidence of an impressive memory. The tyranny of the whole play controlled this teacher's way of thinking, and he controlled the children with his memory, his enthusiasm and his communication skills, the three combined to make up what today is called 'charisma'.

If this advisory teacher was hoping to introduce the children to the essence of the play, I believe he failed. There is a more realistic method that, maybe, requires less of his personality and his prodigious gift of memory, and more of the play's – Shakespeare's – words. Indeed, the man's 'charisma' (as he may well have seen it, secretly) stood between the children and the play. He might have quoted some few lines: '…he unseamed him from the nave to th' chaps' (I:2:23) would have gained full attention, once 'unseamed' was explained; and 'So foul and fair a day I have not seen' (I:3:36) presents a central paradox of the play (compare 'battle won and lost' in I:1:3). Other lines he could have used are 'Is this a dagger?' (II:2:33); 'Unsex me here' (I:5:39); 'Out damned spot' (V:1:30); 'Who's there in th' other Devil's name?' (II:3:6); 'When shall we three meet again/In thunder, lightning or in rain?' (I:1:1); 'The raven himself is hoarse' (I:5:37); 'If it were done when 'tis done, then 'twere well/It were done quickly' (I:7:1–2). All these lines would serve to introduce the play more effectively than the plot (which is Holinshed's anyway) however electrically delivered.

Two comments from correspondents who wrote to me after I had worked in their school on Lady Macbeth's sleepwalking scene (see p. 105) encouraged me. One eleven-year-old boy, Douglas, wrote 'When you read the story about Lady Macbeth's washing her hands, it brought out the real me and gave me a warm heart'. Amanda wrote, 'We had a chance to express how we felt through our work, which doesn't often happen in lessons like science and maths'. This last sentence ought to be written over the door of every politician, civil servant and inspector who is part of a conspiracy, as I write, to downgrade the arts. Either these people do not understand how vital arts are in teaching children about their feelings, or they do see it, but don't want this learning to happen. Why should this be? Are emotionally educated individuals in any way a threat to a society based, not on feelings, but on the cash nexus? Perhaps the traders in the educational temple would be at risk if we were all more honest about our feelings, more stable in our emotions, and less obsessed with our wealth.

Hourd, in her vigorous book, has an account of working with lines from *Macbeth* with young adolescents during the Second World War (1949: 112). She

> gave homeworks (after the first reading of the play, during which the minimum of explanation was given) in which I asked the class to find passages which they felt could be applicable to the present times, and if they could say why…

The results are very affecting now at the end of the century, partly because they are so redolent of the dreadful times in which these children were living. Faced with 'Come what may,/Time and the hour runs through the roughest day' (I:3:146–7) one pupil wrote 'This might be a message of encouragement to us that whatever happens we will go through with it'. 'To offer up a weak, poor, innocent lamb,/To appease an angry god' (IV:3:16–7) provoked one pupil to comment that 'England and France gave Czechoslovakia to Hitler to try and stop a great European war'. 'The labour we delight in physics pain' (II:1:50) refers (says another pupil) 'to the women of today who worry about their relations in the Forces. They lose their thoughts in their work, and therefore delight in it'. This work demonstrates how a previous generation found relevance to their own state in Shakespeare. It should encourage us, as should the whole of Hourd's book which is redolent of the optimism of the progressive movement in education after the end of the Second World War. It is a precursor for much of the creative writing movement of the sixties, and it ought to be reprinted.

There is a contrasting approach to Shakespeare that leads to doggerel. The teacher tells the story and says, 'Be Malcolm'. And we get this, or something like (real example):

> I Malcolm and Donalblain.
> By Macbeth we shall be slain.
> I can feel it in my bones
> Though I am not Sherlock Holmes...

This is still all too common, and often is the result of a less than rigorous engagement with Shakespeare's actual words, and the way they behave. What follows is one way of examining those words carefully. I have said elsewhere in this book that often the most attractive scenes of Shakespeare's plays for children (and, come to that, for many adult readers, including myself) are the scenes that present the pleasures and squalors of low life. This is partly because of their humour, but also (this is mixed up with the humour) they are realistic. The children can recognize them as truthful to human experience and nature more readily than they can recognize the truth in, say, Hamlet's soliloquies and Lear's ravings that are both sane and insane. The Porter's speech in *Macbeth* is a splendid example. Bored, cold, and drunk moving into incipient hangover, he plays a game, pretending he is a porter at the gate of Hell.

The Porter and Hell gate

> Who's there i' th' name of Beelzebub? Here's a farmer, that hang'd himself on th'expectation of plenty...Who's there in the th'other devil's name? Faith here's an equivocator, that could swear in both the scales against either side......Who's there? 'Faith here's an English tailor come hither, for stealing out of French hose. Come in, tailor; here you may roast your goose. Knock, knock! Never at quiet! What are you? – But this place is too cold for hell. I'll devil-porter it no further...
>
> (II:3:1–17)

Children faced with this speech early in their lives will probably never have a fancified idea of Shakespeare as the Bard or the Swan of Avon. They will be immunized early against the sentimental clichés that many use when talking about him and his work. For these reasons I was surprised to find the Porter written out of the adapted version of *Macbeth* used in Gilmour (1997).

I made sure I was in a classroom where the teacher approved of my choice, and I acted this speech to a group of eleven-year-olds. I explained one or two difficulties: for example, French hose is loose, so pieces could be taken from it; an equivocator is a 'juggler with the truth' as Gibson's notes put it; Beelzebub is the devil. Then the class said the speech after me in several ways: rough; whispering; anxious; slurred; sarcastic; sinister; and as humorous as possible; and again, mixing all these effects. I asked the children who they would gladly welcome into a pretend Hell in this game, and they wrote their Porter's speeches, getting going very quickly and working in silence with great enthusiasm.

Before I reproduce these speeches, I'd better say a word about one of what I might call the 'standing orders' I employ. In all the work done by children and presented in this book, there has been silence as they started. I usually tell them that this silence is the only indispensable condition in my study for my writing. And often I ask the children to close their eyes and put their hands over their faces to facilitate it; in particular, to think of the first phrases they are going to write when they start. This does several things: it helps them concentrate; it makes half-sure at least that they've got something to write down when they start; and it produces a healthy working atmosphere. I also try to create a feeling that, in their individual silences, the children should be conscious of playing with words and sentences; of having fun with them, and enjoying their shapes, their sounds and their tastes.

> Knock! Knock! Oh Devil help us who is it this time? Saddam Hussein? You can really blast some nuclear bombs down here. Boom. Crash. Oh come on in, you who puts your lipstick on while driving your car, you can get a scorching makeover down here – through this door to the sauna. Michael Schumacher? You can burn some rubber down here!
>
> (Hannah, 11)

> Knock! Knock. All the time all the time!

> Hullo tax man! Finally down here are 'u'! I thought I'd never see you down here! You can't tax down here! You'll be taxed yourself!

> Knock! Knock! No peace at all, no peace at all!

Oh, hello Mr Policeman! Down in prison yourself! Thought you put people in prison! Serves you right! Always putting other people in the box! Ha! Ha!

Bang! Bang! On the door everyday all day.

Ah! Your majesty! Bah! Down here at last! Always ordering people about!…

Knock! Knock! You never stop do you? Morning noon and night!

Hitler! I was expecting you! Shooting people left right and centre. You're on my list. First world war second world war, makes no difference. Come on in you come!

Ding dong! What? I didn't know we were in the twenty-first century! 'If you wannabe my lover you have got to give'…I'll spice up your life Oh! my ears, my poor, poor ears! Come on in. In you come. You can't sing here. The devil will crush 'u'! Can't sing! Can't dance! Can't do anything! SHUT UP!

Ding!…Oh! I don't know…I'll probably die of loss of water. zzzzzzz (he falls asleep)

(Alice, 11)

I enjoyed this writer's healthy scepticism towards the Spice Girls, and her fortuitous Shakespearean breeziness with history. Another writer wrote 'Ah – a teacher – put your badge with the others'. This is dry and understated. The boy smiled quietly as I read it out, and he glanced at his teacher. The same writer condemned to his Hell 'a white van man – I'll give you roads to rampage along down here' and 'Peter Andre – your plastic pecs will melt down here' (a boy in another school made the same joke about Michael Jackson). Another writer wrote 'Tommy Smith – so the Rector got tired of you at last, did he?' The teacher read this in silence, burst out laughing, and read it to the rest of the class, who cheered, clapped and laughed, much to the delight of the writer. I was the only one who did not understand the joke. Apparently, the Rector took assembly every Tuesday, and each assembly was about a boy called Tommy Smith and his friends, and their tale was linked to something in the Bible. These children had been hearing Tommy Smith stories for seven years.

The Porter's speech from *Macbeth* had allowed one of them to express her feelings about them at last, and had let her become a catalyst for the other children's feelings too. It had allowed her to make a good joke, and to win spontaneous applause for it.

In another school, one boy showed off his knowledge of Lewis Carroll:

> No more slithy toves, Mr Carroll, they're more like burning toves...One and two and through and through, that's what will happen to you down here...
>
> (Glen, 11)

A girl, who 'has no language gifts' according to her gallant teacher, wrote in terms of an old joke.

> Who's there?
> Me.
> Come and sit down with all the other me's...
>
> (Belle, 11)

These strange lines reminded me of Emily Dickinson's poem 'I'm nobody! Who are you?/Are you – Nobody – too?...'. Belle's teacher was 'very surprised' by her writing. Perhaps he needed a little more faith in her, a little more hope, both of which could have been expressed in higher expectations.

This work is vigorous and satirical. It is rare that young writers have an opportunity to attempt satire, and yet we know from their playground rhymes collected by the Opies and others that they have satirical impulses and thoughts. It is also individual: although the children have used the same structure, their content otherwise is different. One poem had a vigour all its own. I left its ungrammatical wrong archaisms because they added to the sheer strangeness of the piece:

> Knock knock knock
> Who be there at the porter's gate of Hell?
> Ah! it is thee who has a heart of stone.
> Thee who hurts.
> Thee who beats.
> Well welcome to the porter's gate of Hell
> And let thy eternal flame burn till
> Till justice burns again.
>
> (Sarah, 11)

Another writer satirized stupidity, first, and then the testing system into which he had been locked since his first day in school at the age of five years.

Idiotic priest, you pressed the wrong button…
Man who invented schools, they'll test you down here.[1]

Later, with a different group of children, I continued the story of this act. In a sense the castle is Hell: the King has been murdered. Macduff yells

Awake, awake!
Ring the alarum bell! Murder and treason!
…
Shake off this downy sleep, death's counterfeit,
And look on death itself! Up, up, and see
The Great Doom's image! Malcolm, Banquo,
As from your graves rise up and walk like sprites
To countenance this horror. Ring the bell!

(III:3:70)

This second group, having just studied through their writing the Porter's grim humour, now said this speech after me, and wrote speeches themselves for someone who has just discovered a dead king. They had commented on the jerky, panicky movement of Macduff's lines:

Get up! Get up! Sound the alarms
Set the sirens wailing, wailing!
You have heard of death, now come and meet him
Shake his hand and look him in the face!
Get up! Set more alarms going!

(Dwayne, 11)

Less melodramatically, one nine-year-old at Newton Linford Primary School in Leicester wrote lines for King Duncan after his murder. I have read them several times: they draw indelible lines between Shakespeare's play and those relationships in the classroom and on the playground to which I referred earlier.

I thought he was my friend,
I though I could trust him.

---

1   Incidentally, teachers responded well to this idea on a course:

How goes the night? Riddled and rapped. With knock knock knock. How goes the night? Ah, my sweetheart inspector. You have graded so many lessons, and now you too have been graded. Come in my sweetness. Less than satisfactory…Hell! Here's a headteacher who sold his soul and his profession and his children on an application form and an accompanying letter. Which part of Hell is best for you, Sir? Here is a writer who believed in the truth of the imagination, but she was prepared to compose worksheets to keep children quiet, because she had to pay her bills. Huh!…

He was loyal to me,
I honoured him.
I thought I knew him,
I thought he loved me.
But I was wrong.

(Gilmour 1997)

Fair and foul: paradoxes

Famously, *Macbeth* is concerned with opposites and even paradoxes. At a casual glance through Act 1, I find easily 'the battle's lost, and won' (I:1:4); 'So foul and fair a day I have not seen' (I:3:36); 'Lesser than Macbeth, and greater' (I:3:63); and 'take my milk for gall' (I:5:46). I pointed this out to some ten-year-old children, and asked them for lines that were 'contradictory'. Among hundreds, they gave me

We are friends and yet we are enemies.

Life is real but at the end it's fake.

Ugly outside pretty inside.

The day was sunny but the sky was dark.

He is faithful but untrustworthy.

The boy looks blind but he can see.

(A lucky commentary on Gloucester in *King Lear*!)

Sun moon, hot cold, light dark, right wrong.

I'm dead but also alive.

The marriage is ahead but also the divorce.

It was the first and last day.

I can be friendly but yet mean.

I have a body but not a spirit.

It seemed like a low life but it was very high.

Life is coming, death is coming.

I have a body without a heart.

God is strong but very weak.

Some of these have a sad factual truth that the writer must have reflected on before in moments of crisis or recall. Here, however, he or she makes that truth into an object worthy of reflection: 'We are friends and yet we are enemies', 'The marriage is ahead but also the divorce'. Others are nearly metaphysical: 'It seemed like a low life but it was very high', 'Life is coming, death is coming'. 'God is strong but very weak' (another lucky commentary, this time on the crucifixion). The writer of 'It was the first and last day' explained it thus: 'A baby has been born, so it's his first day, but his parents don't know he's going to die, so it's his last day as well'. There is more than one way to sentimentalize children: we can, for example, see them as innocents. But we can also see them as uninterested in the huge sad matters of life and death. It is not true. Shakespeare here has given some children a chance to reflect purposefully on some of those issues.

In *Romeo and Juliet*, there is a similar rhetorical trick pulled by Shakespeare. I:1:167–73 and III:2:75 show Romeo and Juliet respectively playing with oppositions. More about this later.

A prose account

I have concentrated throughout on parts of plays and on poetry. Here, though, is an example of a young writer actually engaging with most of a whole play, and writing in excellent prose:

The story from Lady Macbeth's point of view

The letter brought good tidings to me, but the mention of these evil hags was quite upsetting. It made my imagination run wild with thoughts of these fortune-telling wretches, producing such wonderful seeds of the future. However, these thoughts were overrun with thoughts of being Queen. Royalty would fulfil so many of my ambitions for the future. I laid down the letter by my side and called for my servants. They came and I ordered them to prepare for the King and his court's arrival. I dressed myself again in a ballgown with lace, which I thought was appropriate for the occasion.

Macbeth returned victorious from the terrible battle that had taken place between us and the Norwegians. An hour later the King arrived. I read once more the letter and was puzzled. How was Macbeth to be King if Duncan still reigned and has named as his heir to the throne Malcolm? This was our only chance. It may have been murder and treason, but for the crown of Scotland it was worth it. When I first explained this to Macbeth he ignored me and told me to leave. I went deeper into all the details and, with a little encouragement from my side, he agreed to the hideous deed.

The air was cold and crisp along the silent corridor. However the blade in my hand felt like it was burning and needed to accomplish the deed to cool off. I had taken the weapon from one of the guards outside Duncan's room. They were sleeping so deeply that even a stab from the dagger itself would not have woken them up. And fortunately Duncan too was in a deep sleep. I handed the knife to Macbeth and at first he hesitated before I pushed him into the room. I walked slowly behind him. Duncan did not even stir and as the blade plunged into his beating heart I felt a blood-curdling scream deep within me. The deed was done. We may have not walked silently out of the room, but we washed our bloody hands of the dreadful deed.

Morning came, and when I awoke I heard cries of 'Murder, treason, Duncan is dead' I was not shocked, more surprised that the happenings of last night were not just imagination. I ran to the room of death and acted shocked and upset at the King's death. Last night I had remembered to put the dagger back on the guard and had smeared them both with blood to make them appear the guilty party. Macbeth suddenly rushed out and killed the guards. Macduff stared at him. It was a bad mistake. Macbeth poured out how upset he was over King Duncan's death, as an excuse to say why he had killed the guards. I pretended to faint to draw the conversation away from him, as I was running out of reasons why.

Macbeth was made King for Malcolm had fled for fear of his father's death. Macbeth was still unsettled, but, being king, I did not see him much and did not know what terrible things were going to happen. The next day we invited people to a great banquet in our house. Everyone arrived and every seat was filled apart from one stool which Macbeth was to sit on. We all pointed to it, but he would not sit. He said 'How can I sit there when the place is already filled?' 'Nonsense' I said to him, but he still kept on murmuring to himself. I told our guests to leave and said that the King was not well. Macbeth was not coping well with all the guilt, neither was I. Strange visions and phrases overruled my mind and I myself became obnox-ious and angry.

I sat in my room, my hands are covered in blood, and no matter how many times I wash them, they would not come clean. I scrubbed my hands until the skin on them is dry and flaky. In my mind I am walking, walking through a green field. There is a man in front of me. He is singing a song. 'The Thane of Fife he had a wife where is she now?'

(Laura, 11)

This account is memorable for the empathy the writer has achieved for Lady Macbeth (going 'deeper into all the details') and (among some clichés) for many telling images; especially 'wonderful seeds of the future' and the hot dagger desperate to be cooled. Also, that soundless scream is very telling. And the ending is beautifully dreamlike and nightmarish at the same time: the dried, flaky hands and the green field, and the ghostly man singing a folksong: all this conjures up Lady Macbeth's confusion vividly, as do the varying tenses, whether they are intended or not. Note, however, that even here the whole of the play is not used: the Banquo plot has been left out, for example.

Usually, rather than the whole plot, children appreciate the task of looking intensely at one line, and then reflecting on it and developing it.

> Is this a dagger that I see before me,
> A dagger of the hot mind?

(Jonathan, 10)

The witches

Macbeth, then, is wonderfully fertile ground for children writing. Indeed, pastiches, parodies or imitations of the witch's spell in IV:1:1–38 constitute something of a cliché. One teacher, Gina Reid, suggested that I ask children to write a spell for a vegetarian witch, and this freshened the exercise:

> Stinging nettles in the brew,
> Skin of raw potato,
> Left outside for thirty days,
> Rushes shipped from Kilton's pond,
> Orange skin from Kulvatoo,
> Lemon skin from Alcavoo,
> Rotten pears from Mercury,
> Bamboo shipped from Africa,
> A piece of bark from the conga tree,
> A cup of moon juice shipped to me,
> Spiky cactus from Tibet,
> Hang on, it's not finished yet!
> Soggy tomato, in it goes,
> Leaf of poppy, hold your nose,
> Mix it up and when it's done
> Serve the brew to everyone,

(Nicola, 10)

This poem is interesting for at least three reasons. First, teachers often find – I certainly do – that to teach children to write with a formal rhythm is one of the most difficult things to do, and many children only write in free verse. Here, the example of the witches has enabled Nicola to use a formal metre, if a slightly stilted one. This applies to most of the examples here. Second, much as John Betjeman, with his love of brand names – words like 'Timothy Whites and McIlroy's/…MacFisheries…Freeman's' ('Variation on a Theme by T W Rolleston', Betjeman 1958) – knew that such words helped to pin down an era in a poem (1958: 258). Nicola, too, implicitly understands the power of proper names ('Kilton's pond') to sharpen a focus. Third, and probably most importantly, the disgusting subject matter which is sufficiently different from Shakespeare's original, gives these children an opportunity to relish the sound of their language and its meanings.

> Hot and swirling curdling poison,
> Bark of dark dead oak,
> Dripping slimy mud with a spot of ghoul dribble.
>
> Hot and swirling curdling poison,
> Spiny cactus needles stabbing down,
> Black bruised mango head and mushy.
>
> Hot and swirling curdling poison,
> stickling thrushes and stroking brushes,
> slug sucked curdled strawberries poisoned from draper land.
>
> Hot and swirling curdling poison,
> Mushy peas in grey green poison,
> Smashed sharp glass's pointed edge.
>
> Hot and swirling curdling poison,
> A gnat biting flea, tiny and small,
> Old dry flowers crispy as can be.
>
> Hot and swirling curdling poison,
> Clocking ticking, time is wasting,
> time to mix with slimy gravy.
>
> (Aimee, 10)

Aimee has used alliteration, culled from the witches' lines, even though I had not pointed it out to her, or any of the children: 'Bark of dark dead oak,/Dripping...'; 'Black bruised mango'; '...stickling thrushes and stroking brushes...'; 'Clocking ticking, time is wasting, time...'. This shows me something that I have known for decades as a teacher, but acted too rarely on: that children learn things from texts without me as the teacher always teaching them. If we let them play (in the sense of 'amusement...employ oneself in game'), the play (in the sense of 'drama') teaches them. I should act as though I am capable of more faith and hope in the play's pedagogy and the children's abilities and learning, and therefore display less egotistic concern with my own role in that learning. After all, as the Leavisite critic Denys Thompson wrote in a central book of the creative writing movement of the sixties, 'It is a fallacy that what can be learned can and must be taught' (Clegg 1964: xi).

You might say that through the witches, Shakespeare has given spells a bad reputation. Known as 'charms', these are magical poems that have good objectives, and many are collected in Charles Causley's anthology (1974). These children have listened to the witches' spell in *Macbeth*, and been asked to write benevolent versions. The first girl has, like Aimee, used alliteration to musical effect:

> Into my pot I'll throw
> Daisies, dogs, dreams and days.
> Into my pot I'll throw
> Birds, babies, biscuits and bows.
> Into my pot I'll throw
> Animals, air and life.
> Into my pot I'll throw
> music, happiness and life.
> Into my pot I'll throw
> trees and rivers flowing.
> Into my pot I'll throw
> candle light, stars and games.

> (Holly, 10)

One ten-year-old boy wrote all about football, but ended self-deprecatingly 'In it [the ball] goes…As I play around in the bath the bubbles fly as my mum laughs…'. Charlie's poem was quite different from the rest. Although it started as a benevolent spell on his own life, it is what I call a 'good life' poem.

> Have lots of beautiful clothes on Christmas Day
> Be married when you're twenty-two
> Play football for ten years. Be a star
> Have a rainbow over your house every year
> Go on a holiday around the world
> and try not to poo yourself
> Be the King of England on your birthday
> Put the colours of the world into your cauldron
> Go to the golden gates in Heaven
> Die when you are 118 years old

> (Charlie, 9)[2]

2   There is a long tradition of the good life poem in Western European literature: see, for example, Horace's ode number 31 in Book 1 of which there are many fine translations (Shepherd 1983, Michie 1967 will serve for two examples). But Martial has written the poem that Charlie here unconsciously imitates. See Michie (1972) and Porter (1972) for scholarly translations, and here below for part of a casual, unscholarly one – Roeves (1998).

> What's the good life, friend?
> Money handed down, no need to work,
> fair returns for all my effort
> and a house centrally heated without fail;

Such benevolent charms were probably in the majority, but were driven out by the spells, like red squirrels driven out by grey ones. Children can write them with vigour:

Spell for pleasant dreams

Take the gentle hum of a paradise flower
And the low whisperings of a door,
A dew drop of honey
And the smallest pip of the apple core.
Mix them, chop them and grind them up,
Pour them into an acorn cup.
Drink it down while you're in bed
And luxurious thought will enter your head.

(Michelle, 11)

Take the sound of a cat's footfall
A blind man's sight
A deaf man's hearing
And the darkness of light
The beard of a lady
The feet of a snake
Thirteen fishes' wings
And the song of a lake.
Mix them at midnight
With moonlight and dew
And four shining stars
And the potion is through.

(Alice, 10)

To finish, there is a fine spell in 'Shakespeare for Schools', no. 4. Long before the action of *The Tempest*, Ariel is imprisoned by Sycorax in a cloven pine. After hearing this story – versions of which, as Hughes (1992) tells us, play constant variations on a critical theme in mythology, older juniors wrote:

Witches of the world come to me,
Spirits of the world, as bad as can be,

---

rarely having to power dress
in navy suit and floppy bow;
good plain food,
nights sober as possible
with dreams wine-chased away...

(X:47)

Come and get rid of this goodly air,
Make this island bad and bare.
Come from the far corners of the island
Make this island but one dismal desert
Make this island bad and bare.

Out damned spot

Macbeth's immediacy for children was demonstrated clearly and dramatically, at
least to my satisfaction, by an experience I had with sixty ten- and eleven-year-
olds. I read to them the scene where Lady Macbeth sleepwalks (V:1). The
Doctor and the Gentlewomen are watching her, and Lady Macbeth says some of
Shakespeare's most famous lines. These lines mix guilt with terrifyingly clear
memories of the murder; snatches of songs that suggest she is close to the edges
of her sanity with coherent fears of the Hell that the Porter has already prefig-
ured. Most of us find the lines stirring, and despite the horror of what Lady
Macbeth has done, we turn in sympathy to this tragic figure, especially when
she says: '...who would have thought the old man to have had so much blood in
him...all the perfumes of Arabia will not sweeten this little hand' (33–4).
There is much external as well as internal drama here: the scene is not just
about Lady Macbeth's mental or spiritual state. The children realized that Lady
Macbeth is giving away her guilt to the Doctor and the Gentlewoman.

> Out damned spot! Out, I say! – One: two: why then, 'tis time to do't. Hell
> is murky! – Fie, my Lord, fie! A soldier and afeard? – What need we fear
> who knows it, when none can call our power to accompt? – Yet who would
> have thought the old man to have had so much blood in him?...What, will
> these hands ne'er be clean? – No more o'that, my Lord, no more
> o'that...Here's the smell of the blood still. All the perfumes of Arabia will
> not sweeten this little hand...Wash your hands; put on your nightgown;
> look not so pale...To bed, to bed! There's knocking at the gate...What's
> done cannot be undone. To bed, to bed.

The children listened with what I can only call awe, much as the appalled
Gentlewoman and Doctor must have listened. Then, with a simple, traditional
technique that was becoming familiar to me, they read the lines, and then split
them into phrases. I asked them what emotions were going through Lady
Macbeth's mind as she obsessively rubbed her hands, and quickly the children
offered 'guilt', 'regret', 'sadness', 'sorrow' and 'despair'. I then asked them to
write down her thoughts: 'What is going through Lady Macbeth's mind as she
rubs her hands again and again? Write down her thoughts'.

Little was expected of one boy. He rarely achieved much in writing, and, as
his work showed when it was finished, he had considerable difficulties with the
mechanics of writing. Also, he had wriggled on the floor in front of me, as if less

gripped than the rest of the children by the scene. I include here his original spelling to give some idea of his abilities in national curriculum terms, and to demonstrate the difference between his mechanical abilities, and his understanding of this part of the play:

> this booerd well not sweeden even the water forom long rivers
> will not wash it away, I still smell the fresh red blooerd I still can smell it
> like the sweet smell of juicy red plums
>
> It's still there fading
>
> (Sean, 11)

Later, Sean's teacher read this piece to her colleagues. They were surprised at what he had achieved. And yet a first glance at this writing in national curriculum terms would have led to nothing more than concern at bad spelling and more or less non-existent punctuation. Another boy attempted a dialogue between the two sides of Lady Macbeth's personality that he had identified:

> 'God help a poor woman'
> 'It won't come'
> 'in so much sorrow'
> 'We'll be King and Queen together, rich –'
> 'got to wash'
> '–and who will stop us, who would have thought it was'
> 'Oh how pretty the birds in spring'
> 'Save me oh please'
> 'when we feed the ducks'
> 'I can't get rid of it'
> 'Quick let's get out'
> 'oh come out'
> 'They'll never know'
> 'Help!'

Both that boy and another read their lines to the group with remarkable intensity:

> Curse these hands forever stained
> and yet by the fountains of blood from that body,
> that body…curse that moment
> a river of things I could have done
> it had to be the droplet containing death.
> Just do it, do it, do it, do it,
> the pain goes on and on like it can't stop.
> nothing in the world could ever destroy this stain,

a stain no longer on my hand
but in my mind,
my mind now forever cursed.
In hell I will rot in shame, the fire
burning my pure soul

Other individual lines drawn from these writings were:

'Hell rushes through my hands…Ah mould microbes growing on my hands'; 'the king's blood haunting me…his blood is haunting me'; 'guilt is running through my fingers/like out of a tap that will not wash'; 'This liquid will not freshen, I will plunge into the darkness! The red blood stains, internal stains!…Please take pity on my daunted soul!…The King's eyes, fear, pain, as he draws his last breath'

Some teachers will criticize this work for melodrama. 'Aren't these poems' someone remarked 'a fraction over the top?' I concede readily that this is so, and it is true of some other examples in this book. But all writers need to go through a phase of writing in such a way, and it is best to do it when young. Roy Campbell (1930: 34) famously debunked 'certain South African novelists': they wrote with a 'firm restraint…They use the snaffle and the curb all right,/ But where's the bloody horse?' (1930). There are writers like that in every society, including our own. At least in this writing, there is no doubt about the presence of the horse.

Also, it might be said that the writings are all disorganized. But the second two in particular are disorganized in ways that Lady Macbeth's mind is perceived to be. In other words, these boys have used a structure to mirror the state of a mind – without this being an explicit part of my lesson. If my lesson notes had begun with an objective like 'The children will use a structure to mirror the state of a mind' it would have been, obviously, absurdly beyond my scope. But without such an objective (indeed, without any objectives at all) these writers moved some considerable way towards achieving it. Such objectives as I might sensibly have framed would have limited the writing, not increased the possibility of creativity. As the children played, the words of Shakespeare taught them.

Other writers managed powerful figures of speech. Again, 'the children will use original and potent language' would have been a meaningless objective. Examples that did arrive: the microbes on the hands, for example, and the blood 'haunting' Lady Macbeth; the tap that 'will not wash'; the notion of 'internal stains': all these transcended any objectives I might have framed. Incidentally, note the use of 'daunted'. Somewhere Geoffrey Hill uses the word 'maculate' while we are only familiar with its negative form 'immaculate' This writer achieves something of the same effect here.

Chapter 5

Bright smoke
Romeo and Juliet

I have complained before that this play has been seriously hackneyed, and is in danger of becoming the only play that large numbers of a generation know; and also a play that many of that generation will remember merely as a sequence of dull lessons and duller questions of test papers ('I hate that play. We just had to do five pages a lesson when we were doing it for GCSE' said one young man). This state of affairs is shameful: there is so much in *Romeo and Juliet* to teach the young writer. Obviously, children approaching adolescence are interested in incipient love between young people, and this is the central element in this play. The play is also dramatic in its depiction of the violence of Verona's streets (and, by extension, streets anywhere). The way the first scene's violence grows from low-life clowning, through casual, nervous insults, to a fully-fledged brawl, all within a few minutes, is vividly depicted.

We first meet Romeo talking with his friend Benvolio after the street fight which he has missed. He is in love not with Juliet, but with Rosalind, whom we never meet. She does not return his love:

> Why then, O brawling love, O loving hate,
> O anything of nothing first create!
> O heavy lightness, serious vanity,
> Misshapen chaos of well-seeming forms,
> Feather of lead, bright smoke, cold fire, sick health,
> Still-walking sleep, that is not what it is!
> This love I feel, that feel no love in this

(I:1:167–73)

And later Juliet, after she has learned from the Nurse that Romeo has killed her kinsman Tybalt, uses a similar batch of oxymoronic phrases:

> O serpent heart, hid with a flow'ring face!
> …
> Beautiful tyrant, fiend angelical!
> Dove-feathered raven, wolvish-ravening lamb!

Despised substance of of divinest show!
Just opposite to what thou justly seem'st!,
A damned saint, an honourable villain!...

(III:2:73–79)

Indeed, the play, like *Macbeth*, is dotted with opposites like this. Romeo is, as Juliet says, 'My only love sprung from my only hate!' (I:5:137). Shakespeare is fond of oxymorons: two lie on my desk at the moment: 'pale fire' from *Timon of Athens* (IV:3:444), a phrase Vladimir Nabokov used as the title for what to me is the most absorbing novel of the twentieth century; and 'tender churl' from the first sonnet (12). I talked about oxymorons to groups of children, and they proved a powerful way of getting children to avoid clichés and to write fresh phrases that immediately hook the reader. This is a selection from a group of sixty nine- and ten-year-olds, arranged in groups by me. With some of the children, I had time to ask them to take one of their oxymorons and add to it 'to make it even richer':

pleasant war
frightening peace that scares everyone

pointed circle
desert of water
oceanous desert
oasis of sand
a scalding winter
icy sun
solid water
tiny space that seems so big
oh icy lava that's melting

cold warmth
friendly foe
a questioning answer
sad smile
tearful happiness
O moving statue that walks and talks
living death that walks at night
friendly enemy that is so evil
friendly hatred that hurts so much
loudening silence that speaks about you
shouting whisper that can't be heard
pleasurable pain that seems to hurt

The entrance of the exit cannot be escaped
dying life that lives
live for a year and die for a month

beautiful teacher with no hairy legs
lanky fat that's small
vain ugliness

Children in a different school used their oxymorons to compose tiny poems. Some of the writers produced paradoxes with genuine, if fortuitous, insights ('dark snow', for example). Also, these poems, depending as they do on contradictions, more or less prevented clichés by their very nature, and were unusually tight for children's writing:

Fall
  into
    the
      white hole
        of happiness
      then
        you
          will
            live

(Sarah, 9)

Laughing sadness

blunt as a dart
that pricks your finger

fizzy as water

dark as snow

fast as a snail
that goes so slow

short as time
that lasts forever

(Amy, 10)

Unpainful hail but more painful than throwing yourself into a fire
and burning yourself until every bit of your skin goes crispy

(Carl, 10)

There were four broad categories in this work, as I saw it: war, human relations, strange paradoxes and sheer oddities. The oxymorons tumbled upon each other (depending how you look at it) by accident or good luck with a whipping spin on the best of them. Naturally, this technique enabled children to talk about hypocrisy, because all hypocrisy is oxymoronic – a contradiction between the surface and the substance. '...friendly enemy that is so evil' and 'friendly hatred that hurts so much' were telling descriptions that reminded me of money-lenders in Victorian melodrama. For the children of today, these phrases are probably redolent of drug dealers and the publicity surrounding them. One sentence unwittingly recalled *A Winter's Tale* (compare 'O moving statue that walks and talks' with V:3:100ff. when the statue of Hermione moves, and Leontes' sins are forgiven and he is redeemed). '...loudening silence that speaks about you' is about being ignored, or sent to Coventry. Religion and its paradoxes emerged in this writing. 'The entrance of the exit cannot be escaped' is a superb example of a sentence written under the influence of Shakespeare, a great deal of luck, and a natural creativity that children have until it is trained out of them.

Other useful oxymoron appear in *All's Well That Ends Well*, when Helena talks about Bertram, whom she loves:

> His humbling ambition, proud humility,
> His jarring, concord, and his discord, dulcet,
> His faith, his sweet disaster...

> (I:1:146–8)

Romeo's extreme and short-lived love for Rosaline (as expressed to his friend Benvolio) provides a model for following up Demetrius' over-the-top words to Helena in *A Midsummer Night's Dream* (see p. 57) 'a smoke made with the fume of sighs...a sea nourished with loving tears...a madness most discreet,/A choking gall...'. I asked children to write a series of definitions – almost a kenning – for love and hate.

Love

blood-pumper
palm-sweater
dream-filler
meaning-giver
long-laster

Hate

home-breaker
death feeling
fiery heart
clenched body

In the last of the love kennings, there was a lucky reference to Sonnet 116: '...love is not love/Which alters when it alteration finds,/Or bends with the remover to remove./O no, it is an ever-fixed mark...'

Queen Mab

As I came towards the end of the project, I worked on Mercutio's Queen Mab speech with a group of seven children:

> O then I see Queen Mab hath been with you:
> The fairies' midwife, and she comes
> In shape no bigger than an agate-stone
> On the forefinger of an alderman,
> Drawn with a team of little atomi
> Over men's noses as they lie asleep.
> Her chariot is an empty hazel-nut,
> Made by the joiner squirrel or old grub...

After more about Queen Mab and her chariot, we come to the part of the speech that tells us what she gets up to:

> ...she gallops night by night
> Through lovers' brains, and then they dream of love,
> O'er courtiers' knees, that dream on curtsies straight,
> O'er lawyers' fingers, who straight dream on fees,
> O'er ladies' lips, who straight on kisses dream,
> Which oft the angry Mab with blisters plagues
> Because their breaths with sweetmeats tainted are...
>
> (I:4:54–93)

Because the speech is so long, rich and detailed, I gave every child in the group a copy, and we read it several times, playing the games that the reader will be familiar with by now: saying the speech phrase by phrase altogether and in groups; the children filling in words that I'd missed out; varying the tone from humorous to sinister; the pace from fast to slow; changing pitch and volume; emphasizing the unpleasant words, like 'sluttish', 'blisters' and 'plagues', or the pleasant ones, like 'moonshine's watery beams', 'lovers' and 'kisses'; reading violently or sarcastically or wonderingly. After swapping our lines around, we read it a few more times until many of the phrases were planted in the children's heads. I suggested that Queen Mab was not the sort of fairy, frail and fey, that a hoaxing Victorian photographer might have snapped at the bottom of his garden, that could be swatted by a rolled-up newspaper. She is tough, ruthless and resourceful. I then asked children to write their own Queen Mab speech:

O then I see Queen Mab has been with you:
She is the trees' bark shaper, and she comes
In a shape as round as our earth itself,
A small particle of magical fate,
Travelling, floating with the natural breeze.
Through polar bears' hairs she explores the ice.
Her spherical carriage gracefully soars
Looked on by inhabitants, young and old,
Infinite omens and curses are chanted:
The portholes in her sphere of glistening webs,
Her seat inside of shining beetle's shell,
Her silk jacket red as Jupiter's glow,
Her jewels of water shoes of tropical heat,
Her chauffeurs red-jacketed wire-haired dogs,
Abyssinian, native bred, small kings.

(Lizbeth, 11)

This girl's mind is always thick with ideas and her work has a rare richness, a fluent random quality, as we can see from her account of Bernard arriving at his wedding on p. 87. The lack of consecutive argument in this piece does not matter at all; nor does the shaky punctuation. By looking at and visually studying the Mab speech, Lizbeth has internalized some qualities of iambic pentameters. Now, as I finish this book (I don't write from beginning to end, but in the order that seems right at a given time) I reflect that if I were starting now, I would give more of the children the chance to look intensively at Shakespeare's words, instead of just hearing and tasting them.

Through poet's brains she gallops
as they dream of quotations and rhyming couplets
Through writers' brains she walks slowly
marvelling at all the towering bookshelves...
She finds an old man
in hospital
and in his mind are
photo albums and memories
and he is dreaming that his wife
will come and take him from this earth...

(Jack, 11)

Chapter 6

Furious winter's rages

King Lear and *Cymbeline*

King Lear is traditionally seen as one of the most difficult of the plays. It is, indeed, a massive understatement to say that it is emotionally complex and profoundly disturbing. But an anecdote from the American playwright Arthur Miller (1987: 59–60) implicitly warns us never to assume that the relatively unlettered – in his case his father, in our case the children we teach – can't get something from even the most difficult text. Miller senior would normally not sit through any Shakespeare, but he'd come across a Yiddish production of a play, the name of which he couldn't remember, of which 'the great Joseph Adler' was the star:

> He played some kind of king. You know, it was the olden days. And he had three or four daughters....And he's going to give each one some of his money, and the one that really loves him the most he thinks don't love him. So he ends up half out of his mind looking for his buttons, and he's got nothin' and he's left there standing in the rain....I seen that show, must've been over forty times...he's out there in the rain. He would belt out a roar that you couldn't bear to look at him...

That story should be a lesson for those of us too ready to assume only the easy is good for children and old people who've never read Shakespeare. Miller senior supplies a succinct commentary on Lear's last words (V:3:279–84: 'Never, never, never, never, never./Pray you, undo this button. Thank you, sir./Do you see this? Look on her! Look, her lips...') when he says Lear is 'out of his mind looking for his buttons'!

However, neither *King Lear* nor *Cymbeline* offers anything like as many ideas for writing as any of the plays I've written about so far. But although it is true that *A Midsummer Night's Dream*, *Macbeth* and *Romeo and Juliet* lead the field as teachers of writing among Shakespeare's plays, each of the others has hidden surprises. One speech in *King Lear* presents children with opportunities to express parts of their personalities that are usually hidden in the classroom – to belt out a roar, and unlike many of the speeches I have used, this one is a crucial one made of famous lines. I explained how Lear had lost the only daughter who loved him; how he had been treated by the other daughters; and about how he was now at the mercy of the 'pitiless storm'. When dealing with the wider context of a play like this, it is important to be as spare as possible; to sketch no more than the necessary facts; to be, unlike the teacher I quoted in the section about *Macbeth*, minimalist. In fact, Miller senior's summary of the plot is exemplary. I then read 'Blow winds', imagining a formidable American Jew in the 1920s, Joseph Adler:

> Blow, winds, and crack your cheeks! rage! blow!
> You cataracts and hurricanoes, spout
> Till you have drench'd our steeples, drowned the cocks!
> You sulphurous and thought-executing fires,
> Vaunt-couriers to the oak-cleaving thunderbolts,
> Singe my white head!...

(III:2:1–6)

I explained the difficult words using *The Cambridge School Shakespeare:King Lear* (Bain, Morris and Smith 1996). Cataracts and hurricanoes are waterfalls and waterspouts, 'thought-executing' means mind-numbing and 'vaunt-couriers' are forerunners. However, some of the children had understood several of these meanings, partly I suspect because of my reading, but more, I believe, because of the context: other words that they already understood: 'blow', 'rage', 'drench' and 'thunderbolt'. They said the speech after me in different ways. I asked them to write a call to the weather telling it to do its worst in a style like that of Lear's speech. I said they could be as free as they liked to write terrible things. I had not tried the idea up to this point. What happened next surprised me as much as anything in the course of this project. I was not prepared for the violence of the children's writing, nor for the fact that the most violent imagery came from girls. In the end, I was glad to see two persistent stereotypes wobbling again: innocent children and gentle girls. I print the first piece exactly as Shona wrote it.

> weather, dry the earth so its as dry as a bone so the worlds a desert. Kill all living things on earth, kill country by country dry up all the lakes, rivers, dry up all the drops of water, dry up the sea, so the worlds made of sand, then lightning burn the deserts, burn the houses to an ash, burn the people who did not suffer, burn the world to an ash.

(Shona, 8)

This writer told me later that she had moved to her school in Berkshire the previous year from Perth, Australia, and I can feel and see Australia in this writing. I can also feel an extraordinarily delighted relish in the repetition of words describing the horror. This turned out to be typical of the work done in this session:

Clouds of rain burst like balloons,
Trees blow over from the storm.
Creatures curl up and die,
Make the weather go mad,
Make the world die and all the planets crash.
God destroy us please
Planes fall into the sea
And universe be destroyed,
Good bye world forever!

(Sophie, 8)

I enjoyed the way in which Sophie had taken the image in Shakespeare's 'Blow winds and crack your cheeks' and adapted it to her first line about the balloons. Again, the writer dealt with chaos with delight. It was safe for her to do so and was a kind of dummy run for any chaos that might (God forbid) afflict her in real life. The next writer had a candid first line, a blunt and frightening instruction, a roar belted out indeed:

Violence begin with the weather.
Lightning do your terrible storms.
Drown all the houses like a river,
crash and storm the roofs off houses.
Defeat the trees.
Do the heaviest rain.
Wind, blow all the sheds over all the world.
The lands will be flooded. Dead people floating in the water,
seas ripping apart.

(Zoe, 8)

In the final example, the writer used animals to show up her chaos:

horses horses everywhere
as they walk they kick they boot they buck
they kick their stables
as the farmers do their farming
they see their sheep laying and dying
we are the animals of God
but we will not be there for long.
next comes lightning crashing trees
they don't even have a time for prayering
and now we bash and bang
hiding behind a tigers thang
theres bashing banging everywhere oh world
dont let us die

the floods are coming in
and it will soon go dry
o wind
o trees do not fall on me

(Anon, 8)

Someone will say that this writing (especially in the fourth, anonymous piece)
is disorganized, but that unfinished feel is vital to it, as it was to the accounts of
Lady Macbeth's sleepwalking on pp. 106–7. The writers implicitly understand
that in writing about chaos they can employ chaos. For the teacher to tidy it up
in any way – grammatically, in terms of punctuation or in terms of any sense of
order and tidiness at all – would be to miss the point. This is often true of children's writing in less dramatic ways: the helter-skelter rush of sentences without
full stops speaks of a breathless emotion as much as it speaks of an ignorance of
punctuation (see Sedgwick 1994:48 for an example of this).

I learned, or rather re-learned, an important truth from this writing. Our
relationship to the environment in all its moods is elemental. We are drawn to
the sea at least in part because millions of years ago we were drawn from it. The
term 'sun-worshipper' may be facetious, but it also contains an element of truth.
It hardly needs saying that in *King Lear* the storm and his response to it are
paralleled by the storm that is in his head. These pieces of children's writing are
vivid and disturbing examples of our intimate relations with nature. They speak
of the violence and the fascination with violence that is in all of us. If the
poetry of Ted Hughes is, at least in part, an unremitting, unrepentant glare at
the savagery implicit in humankind's relations with the world, these poems are,
in comparison, little, honest glances.

The obscurity of the Lear speech did not matter in the end. As the children
listened to it, they internalized more than most adults would have predicted.
Indeed, they learned it not so they could say it without books – that is a relatively
minor kind of learning – but so that they could use it to make their own poems,
and so they could wrestle with it later that day, that term, that year, that life.

Other possible lines from Lear that readers might try with suggested tasks are:

Sir, I love you more than word can wield the matter…

(I:1:50)

Write a poem made up of flattery, of exaggerated love, from one daughter or son
to his/her father or mother. Perhaps there is an ulterior motive, money in a will,
for example.

–Nothing.
–Nothing?
–Nothing will come of nothing. Speak again.

(I:1:82–5)

–This is nothing, fool.
–Then 'tis like the breath of an unfeed lawyer; you gave me nothing for 't.
Can you make no use of nothing, uncle?

(I:4:113–5)

I am a fool, thou art nothing

(I:4:153)

Write a poem in which all the negative words ('nothing...no...nil...naught...
no-one...nobody...') figure. A thesaurus will come in useful.

For by the sacred radiance of the sun,
The mysteries of Hecate and the night,
By all the operation of the orbs
From whom we do exist and cease to me;
Here I disclaim all my paternal care...

(I:1:103–7)

Write five lines, ten syllables in each, that make up an oath. What would you
swear by? Things to do with learning and school? ('For by the sacred blackboard
and the great/Green playing fields, the dingy changing rooms/For by the goal I
scored in extra time/Against St Matthew's Prep to win the game/For by the
glint in the mad headteacher's eye/And the smile in Miss Smith's when she
praises Sam/I say 'That was my chip, that my fish finger...')

Fear no more the heat o' the sun: a song from *Cymbeline*

At the beginning of this book, most of the poems I published were cheerful in
tone. *A Comedy of Errors*, *A Midsummer Night's Dream*, *As You Like It*, even *The
Tempest*: all these invited humour and an optimistic way of looking at life. The
mood darkened of course with *Macbeth* and *King Lear*. Here, I ask children to
reflect on death in less problematical, more ordinary ways. I had neither read
nor seen *Cymbeline* until I started this book. This is a lesson for me at least –
never assume that what is not as famous as the big names is unworthy of a closer
look. To read *Cymbeline* as an adult not knowing what would happen was an
unusual pleasure. Imagine reading your favourite novel: *Pride and Prejudice*,
perhaps, *Jane Eyre*, or *Brighton Rock* without the knowledge all the way through
of who ends up with whom.

The first time I worked with children on the song 'Fear no more the heat o'
the sun', I simply read Guiderius' and Arviragus' lovely duet-lament for the
supposedly dead Fidele/Imogen, and asked them to write poems beginning with
the same three words for animals that had died.

Fear no more the heat o' the sun,
  Nor the furious winter's rages,
Thou thy wordly task has done,
  Home art gone and ta'en thy wages.
Golden lads and girls all must,
  As chimney-sweepers, come to dust.

Fear no more the frown o' the great,
  Thou art past the tyrant's stroke,
Care no more to clothe and eat,
  To thee the reed is as the oak:
The sceptre, learning, physic, must
  All follow this and come to dust.

Fear no more the lightning-flash.
  Nor th' all-dreaded thunder-stone.
Fear not slander, censure rash.
  Thous hast finish'd joy and moan.
All lovers young, all lovers must
  Consign to thee and come to dust...

                                   (IV:2:268–75)

This was a crude approach to a beautiful poem, but it paid ample rewards which made me reflect immediately on how much richer writing would be with a little more sensitive preparation. This exercise also demonstrated that play does not mean triviality. Here the children play with the biggest riddle of all, death:

Zebra

Fear no more of the lion roar.
Fear no more of the beastly gun.
Fear no more of starvation in winter
Fear no more in the ferocious grasslands
Fear no more of cuts and bruises
Fear no more of the bang of thunder and the flash of lightning.

                                   (Daniel, 9)

'The ferocious grasslands' struck me as a genuine line: true and fresh with no hint of a cliché about it, and yet with enough of familiar phrases ('the killing fields') to avoid obscurity. None of the other poems in this session managed quite such a delicate balance (though I would say that 'loud bright thunder' comes close in a different way), but all were moving:

Tiger

Fear no more the aiming from an arrow.

Fear no more the collar round your neck.
Fear no more the feeling of following humans.
Fear no more the rain and no shelter.
Fear no more the hunting for your fur.
Fear no more the killing for your cubs.
Fear no more the going down on food.
Fear no more the loss of the neighbour's home.
Fear no more people running after you.
Fear no more the snow wind and rain.
Fear no more of something coming.

(Emily, 9)

Dolphin

Fear no more the dread of pollution, cans scattered in the waters, man and
his cruelty to you, the dread of starvation, fear nothing

(Kate, 8)

Cat

Fear no more the roar of an up-coming car...
Fear no more the tick of the hour...
Fear no more an eternal chase.
Fear no more the last breath of your weary body...

(Mark, 9)

Horse

Fear no more
    the
        loud
           bright
              thunder
   the
      slithery
        scary
          snake
            that
              bites
 and
      wicked
        people
         out
          in
           the

                                                    world
          all these things you do not have to fear
          for God will look after you in Paradise forever

                                                    (Sarah, 8)

    Notable lines from other work in this session included 'fear no more the
howling of a wolf as gray as dust' (to an ape) and 'the cars chasing you round
swerved corners…the dark nights in the pet shop.' (to a cat)
    What can we say about the children's learning as they wrote these poems?
First, the children had obviously appreciated the power of Shakespeare's phrase,
as they were able to use it with great effect themselves. Thus, in their writing-
play they were learning about the poetry of Shakespeare. Second, they invented
unusual phrases, notably the ones I have picked out for comment already, but
also 'cans scattered in the waters', 'the tick of the hour' and 'the dark nights in
the pet shop'. Thus, through a close engagement with Shakespeare's song
(though, not as I will show, as close as it might have been) they have learned
about their language and the power if it. Third, the children have reflected on
major issues that did not concern Shakespeare and his contemporaries. For
example, Sarah is reflecting on the horror of physical attacks on horses, which
was in the news at the time, and Kate is thinking about pollution. Fourth, and
probably most importantly, the children are learning about their own worries.
By using the animals as subjects they have been able to distance themselves
slightly from these worries, but the adult reader can see them clearly.
    This is most evident in Emily's last line: 'Fear no more of something coming';
and Mark's line about the 'tick of the hour' – a marvellous 'rinsed cliché' (to use
Christopher Ricks' elegant phrase about Geoffrey Hill); and possibly in 'Fear no
more people running after you' (Emily).
    I played to another group of children Bryn Terfel's performance of Gerald
Finzi's marvellous setting of this song (1995).

          Fear no more
          he never walks away
                and leave
                   you

          Fear no more
          no more cholic
                and
          laminitis
             for you

          Fear no more
                pain
          Fear no more
                Fear no more

> no more uneasy
>   times now to have in
>   the life

Later, other children played in the same way with this song and wrote, respectively, about a grown-up cousin and a grandmother:

> Fear no more the morning rain
> Fear no more the beautiful clothes you used to wear
> Fear no more the dreadful illness that you did suffer
> Fear no more the worrying loss of money
> Fear no more the life that you had in your earlier days
> Fear no more the loss of Ken
> Fear no more your caring life and the air that you breathe
> Fear no more the thundering storms
> Fear no more how much I loved you
> Fear no more your great big family
> Fear no more the afternoon's rain
> Fear no more your eyes are shut
>
> (Melissa, 10)

> Fear no more, the knitting's done.
> Fear no more, the garden's growing.
> Fear no more, the thunder's blown away.
> Fear no more, the toad's OK.
> and is still mucking the leaves.
> Fear no more, your son's teddy's safe.
> and all your possessions are in good hands.
> Fear no more the heart attacks and hospitals.
> Fear no more, the blackberries are picked
> and the jam tarts are done.
> Fear no more, Grandad's well.
> Fear no more of amusing me.
>
> (Anna, 10)

It is unusual for children to be offered in school either the opportunity to face up to such shocking realities – 'the dreadful illness that you did suffer', 'the worrying loss of money', 'the heart attacks and hospitals', 'the loss of Ken' – or to express so frankly such love: 'how much I loved you'. It is teaching Shakespeare that has achieved this.

One other, rather less elevated possibility for writing in *Cymbeline* are the lines that Guiderius uses when he enters with Cloten's head:

This Cloten was a fool, an empty purse,
There was no money in 't: not Hercules
Could have knock'd out his brains, for he had none...

(IV:12:113–15)

I suggested that the same children might write an epitaph for a fool, and offered my own example: 'He was a drawer full of bent paperclips/and old torn photographs of interest/to no-one but himself;/Of dry-nibbed topless/pens, flat batteries...' One boy wrote:

He's a hurricane with no wind!
He's like the sea with no waves!
He's like a lion with no guts!
He like a football with no air!
He's like a soul with no emotion!
He's like a mouth with no tongue!
He's like trousers with no flies!

(Douglas, 10)

That is all about children writing, except for an afterword. We move now to a short section on learning Shakespeare by heart.

Chapter 7

By heart

The children who have contributed their writing to this book have been learning Shakespeare in a more potent way than some other approaches allow.

Playing with one's own words in response to Shakespeare's by writing is more educational than say reading plays in the class ('Now, Sedgwick, you'll be Mistress Quickly'), or poring over them for the purpose of passing tests or examinations ('Just get some quotations into your heads, that's what matters'). 'After an exam-warped education too many children leave school unaware of and uninterested in their own literature' (Denys Thompson in Clegg 1965: x). What he wrote is as true then as it is now. Scarily, it is more relevant because the system has become more riddled with tests than it was in the sixties.

The power of what children learn when they play with Shakespeare's words derives from the fact that play, being active, is bound up with choice: playing with words requires constant decisions. Decisions require thought and thought causes that dangerous thing – learning – about Shakespeare, about words, about life and its glories and problems. About, amongst other things, its squalor. In contrast, the dull business of reading and swotting for exams requires little more than a numbed, passive response remembered in later years, if remembered at all, as a chore. Also, and this is worse for the student (or so I remember, and so other people have told me) such activities seem to be utterly cut off from any recognizable aspects of real life.

This chapter is about learning Shakespeare in a particular and (in my view) limited sense of the word, though it is the only sense in many people's experience. Before I enter the debate about heart and rote learning, I have to say that through the active language *play* that I have described up to this point in my book, many of the children became so familiar with parts of the *plays* (the repetition of the word may sound awkward, but, as I've implied before, it is a significant pun) because they enjoyed them so much. The words went directly into their brains and hearts and stayed there. This was sometimes through deliberate effort, but sometimes it was more natural. One day I heard infants on a playground at lunch-time calling out 'I'll follow you' to each other, and chasing each other in a game of tag. They ran, crept, crawled under, over and through slides and climbed frames saying the versions of Shakespeare's lines from A

Midsummer Night's Dream (III:1:87–94) that they'd just written with me in class, and sometimes Shakespeare's own lines. I was impressed by how many of the children had memorized many of the lines in Puck's speech.

Watching them made me realize that between us we could invent games for learning. Another speech from *A Midsummer Night's Dream* that I have used, 'Now the hungry lion roars' (V:1:349–68), is the useful subject of such a game that I have invented and will play one day. After working with the speech for writing purposes (see p. 60) a class of children will sit in a circle. The first person will say 'Now it is the time of night'. The next person must then say any line he or she can remember from Puck's speech. If a mind goes blank (this will happen less and less as the game goes riotously on), 'Now it is the time of night' or 'Now the hungry lion roars' must be repeated. And so on and so on round the circle. I will do the same with 'Fear no more the heat o' the sun'. After a writing lesson, I'll revert to the original and say the main phrase while pointing to children in the circle, who will have to say one of Shakespeare's other phrases. This will work with any of the speeches in Shakespeare that have repetitions in them. Some speeches, of course, like 'Fear no more' require more reverence than others, though no precocity.

On some occasions, I suggested that children who had written about a certain passage should deliberately try learning it by heart, and many children succeeded. Eleven-year-olds rushed up to the gate of one village school in Suffolk as I arrived one morning, chanting gleefully Gertrude's lines about the death of Ophelia. On another occasion in Berkshire, I had challenged the oldest children to learn the Porter's speech from *Macbeth*. Judging from the sarcasm and abuse hurled at me as I got out of the car ('Who's there i' the name of Beelzebub!…Come in equivocator') the children had taken my challenge to heart.

By heart learning, or learning that springs from the kind of experiences these children were having, is often confused with 'rote learning'. However, the two things are quite different from each other. Rote involves a 'mechanical manner…routine…the mere exercise of memory without proper understanding of, or reflection upon, the matter in question…' (*Shorter Oxford English Dictionary*). William Cowper writes somewhere that 'Words learn'd by rote a parrot may rehearse'. An ex-grammar school pupil said to me:

> We had to learn 'Once more unto the breach…' on pain of detention…I still like the words, very much. Whenever I think of the speech, it's changed a bit for me. In those days it was like a war effort, that patriotic Olivier approach…you know, 'God for Harry, England and St George!' and praiseworthy. But then in those long gone days I used to stand for the national anthem when the film finished!…It now seems to be about the violence of the state…That cannon face isn't very human…I've never actually seen that very clearly…'Let it pry through the portage of the head…'

Another ex-grammar school pupil said:

> I remember having to learn a great long speech at the beginning of *Henry IV Part I*…[quotes solemnly and inaccurately] 'So shaken as we are with toil and care Find we a place for frighted peace to pant'. It seemed dull and convoluted. I never got the point, and no-one ever told me, that it's meant to be like that, till you told me just now, that Henry IV is a worried, convoluted man….That bloody speech more or less destroyed Shakespeare for me….I could say it for years like a parrot, without really understanding any of it…

If those two were ambivalent and downright dubious respectively about the value of rote learning, three correspondents spoke up for it. An anthologist for schools said:

> I remember learning some of the songs with a student teacher, I think it was….I think it went down like a lead balloon, rough working class kids in London…, 'Full Fathom Five', 'When greasy Joan doth keel the pot'….I remember having some fun with the old-fashioned s's in 'Where the bee sucks', we must've had a facsimile of the original, and I think we had a few laughs about that at the teacher's expense….But there are better ways of doing it today, more of a carrot than a stick thing…making it a bit of fun….It's good for children because it teaches them about the iambic pentameter…

The point about Shakespeare's characteristic use of this line is extended by an unpleasant character in a novel by A S Byatt who says 'the iambic pentameter embodies…the number of heartbeats between a breath taken in and the same breath sighed out…' (1978: 415). Much as the beat of certain popular songs represents the heartbeat, or multiples of it, the iambic pentameter is the natural line of English speech. Therefore, my anthologist might argue, Shakespeare is ideal for learning. I have already suggested that there are better, more active ways of learning the iambic pentameter that involve saying it and writing it.

An education lecturer said:

> I had to learn Shakespeare by rote when I was 14, large parts of *Hamlet*, and I am glad I did! I can still remember the taste of the words in my mouth. We should have done rote learning in the 60s and 70s but we didn't because it wasn't in tune with the dominant ideology of the time….I was a progressive because that is what you were, but I asked children, on the quiet, to commit lines of poetry to memory and say them in assembly….Like I got them to learn their tables! We should've argued that there's a place for that sort of thing.

Another lecturer was grateful for her own school-enforced rote learning, but had not encouraged it as an infant teacher and headteacher:

> We had to learn poems off by heart…it was one thing you could be left safely to do when the teacher was out of the room. I once learnt the whole of 'Lepanto', I've still got chunks of it….I'm glad I did it, I'm all for it….When I was a teacher children learned songs and plays, but no, I didn't go big on it…

I thought there was a contradiction here: if learning by heart was good for her as a child, why not for the children she had taught? She said:

> Although for me it began in a classroom, it was really a private thing….I did it to get *out* of the classroom….I wouldn't want to impose rote-learning on children in infant schools today…

Another correspondent echoes that. 'The poems I had to learn weren't the ones I love now. The ones that matter to me now I internalized by myself'. Reflecting on that afterwards, I recalled my own experiences. I acquired most of the poems I know off by heart in a few minutes each without really trying when I was young. Only three of these are by Shakespeare: sonnets 18 ('Shall I compare thee to a summer's day?'), 129 ('The expense of spirit in a waste of shame') and 130 ('My mistress' eyes are nothing like the sun'). I have written about my by heart learning elsewhere:

> I have spent many happy solitary hours walking country lanes, beaches and city streets thinking of whole poems and saying them to myself: 'The More Loving One' by Auden…is a perfect poem for saying on country lanes on clear nights in summer, much as Yeats' 'The Wild Swans at Coole' should be kept for autumn days near water.
>
> (in Wilson (ed.) 1998: 22)

and I realized that the private aspect of this was very important to me too. Poems got by heart were not for chanting in school, their rhythms debased to a clock's tick-tock, and certainly not for impressing anyone (an unlikely thought anyway). They were for taking on in the silence of my own room, my own head and my own heart, and for using under the stars or by autumn streams on solitary walks, or on Westminster Bridge, oblivious of the rush hour. They had a quasi-religious function. They helped me to keep in touch with the truths in poets' heads that might be my truths or parents to my truths. Their rhythms became mixed up with the rhythms of my walk: they thus became truly mine. They became part of my stock of 'weapons of war against brutality and darkness' (Picasso's phrase, I believe).

Getting by rote, painfully or otherwise, long tracts of blank unrhymed verse is one way of learning Shakespeare's lines. But it is different from what I have described earlier. The first problem (apart from the pain) is that it is hit and miss. It is true that some adults are grateful that they have had those lines pressed into their heads in their teens on pain of various punishments ranging from smacks to detention. For them, the lines' meanings grow and change with the years, and they are able to treasure those lines and the slow organic change of the meanings of those lines in their head. This is, incidentally, much as our allegiances to characters grow: when we first come across *Romeo and Juliet*, we are Romeo or Juliet; a few years later we are Tybalt or Mercutio; then the Capulet or Montague parents; and eventually we are the Nurse or the Friar. But the plays go on living with us in another way, much as my first correspondent has suggested. We re-interpret the militarism of the speech at Agincourt as we grow older. We may start by seeing Lear as cruelly hard done by, but eventually alter our perspective and see events from Regan and Goneril's point of view. Later still, understandably, we might revert to Lear. We warm to Caliban and see him not as a savage, but as a victim of colonialism. And then we notice the beauty of his verse: can this person really be a savage? I can accept that rote learning helps some people to grow in their understanding of Shakespeare's characters.

Most, though, are not so lucky. Most of us remember the tedium of committing words to memory – words that, apparently, bore no relationship to our own lives. To us, the rote-learning was like chewing tasteless meat we didn't ask for and don't want. Indeed, rote learning, school dinners and long games afternoons in the winter are bracketed together in many minds. The 'thees and thous', at the lowest level, irritated and continue to irritate such readers, much as lumpy spuds infuriated us and the heaving and heading of a heavy wet lump of leather in what was cynically called 'training' wore us down. 'There can be no value at all in having read *Coriolanus* at the expense of acquiring a total aversion to Shakespeare' says Flower, and he is right (1966: 174). Similarly, there is no value in gaining by rote any numbers of lines if we remember them now with boredom and resentment, or worse.

Shakespeare's characterisation, achieved through the medium of blank verse, baffled many reluctant Shakespeare students (as it baffled many in the first group who managed to stay with Shakespeare: they just struggled on for various reasons). The Elizabethan diction and the complex sentence construction put them off as well. These people will have none of the idea that rote-learning is in some way character-building. It merely created, as Ted Hughes has written, 'an aversion to learning and to poetry'. It made them feel like parrots. So why subject young people to this business?

A traditional case for learning Shakespeare by rote is that the speeches and poems will become what one of my correspondents called 'touchstones' throughout life. We will be able to 'revisit' any lines we learn at will. He had been talking to some women in their seventies and eighties who had 'sentimental poems like "I remember, I remember", "I think that I shall never see....A poem lovely as a tree", stuff like that, off by heart...and those poems meant so much to them'. The first of my two educational lecturers, it turned out, had been a fifth-columnist formal teacher in her sixties salad days. Although she had dressed her school and her reputation in the clothes of a thorough-going progressive, all hessian displays, double-mounting and Plowdenesque child-centredness, she told me:

> Poems and speeches, especially by Shakespeare, that you have off by heart are lovely to recall. I love their cadences and their musicality. I can have them at will in my private time....I love that sense of power, you have with someone else's words inside you. I think you defend rote learning because of the beauty of the words. It's an aesthetic thing...and it's really nice to be able to quote them at dinner parties!...

I was troubled by the sub-Arnoldian notion of 'touchstones' – as though certain works had an objective reality, solid as rocks, that allowed them to be elevated to a quasi-scriptural status. This was too much like the Grecian-urning that I described in my introduction. To come to terms with art viewed in such a way we only have to be passive receivers of its wisdom and grace, which effectively means passive receivers of some interpreter's version of that wisdom and that grace. There was, too, a disturbing discrepancy between 'I remember, I remember' (for all that I'd used it with children on many occasions as a writing stimulus), 'Trees' and, say, a Shakespeare sonnet. If the notion of 'touchstones' is so elastic, it can't be worth much. Another part of the case is that it 'teaches children the iambic pentameter'. But Lizbeth (p. 113) has learned about this more effectively by reading some iambic pentameter lines intensively and writing in imitation of them: again, active as opposed to passive learning. Learning by rote (it is further asserted) helps in the development of memory skills. And, nearly all my correspondents agreed, such learning is much easier when you are young. Therefore, we should (the argument continues) 'cash in' (a revealing usage from one of my correspondents) while it is still possible.

It can be said with some confidence that rote learning is useful when there is a point to it that the children can see as well as the teacher. The decision though can be taken, and these confident views expressed by adults only; the children can have no say in them. And sometimes children misunderstand the purposes, and sometimes they subvert them. An extreme example of the idiocy of learning by rote and its more negative effects can be found in an article by Mordecai Rosenfeld (1998). After memorising 'Trees' in Grade Five, along with poems by Robert Service (of 'Dangerous Dan McGrew' fame), he and his classmates were told to learn a Shakespeare sonnet, Number 29 ('When in Disgrace with Fortune and Men's Eyes'). The leap that this process entailed must have been baffling, and rather like, in today's terms, moving in musical appreciation from the school choir singing 'Joseph and his Amazing Technicolored Dreamcoat' (again) to hearing Janet Baker singing Strauss's 'Four Last Songs', or

Louis Armstrong's 1928 recording of 'West End Blues'. In any case, from the ensuing account it is clear that however much pain Rosenfeld and his class-mates (and, come to that, his teachers) suffered, it was nothing compared to what the poem went through. After a week or two allowed for committing it to memory, each pupil had to say it in front of the class in turn. They were then graded: 100 per cent for no errors at all, and so on downwards.

What a lesson that must have been if you were reader number 30 out of 30 with an unfair advantage in terms of the task in hand. Hearing your classmates do the job must have been a great help if you were called Zemblinsky, and a profound gloom brought on by the meaningless repetition (I bet Zemblinsky never read the sonnets again). You would be committing it deeper into your memory as you heard your mates doing their bit, but (as though you would have cared at that age) the slow destruction of its emotional and intellectual effect must have been dramatic. While the girls said the poem 'Con Amore' ('disgusting' Rosenfeld assures us, and I believe him), the boys, demonstrating the power children possess to subvert much of the pointlessness of school life, held a secret competition to discover who could say the poem fastest. The 'Con Amore' readings may well have been attempts at subversion as well.

The better-off boys had Mickey Mouse watches with sweep hands and they timed everyone. 'In order to win…you had to blurt out the entire sonnet in one breath. Any pit stop – for a sneeze, a sniffle, a cough, a wheeze, an itch, a grimace, a toothache, a frown, and idle thought – was fatal'. Rosenfeld's mother was understandably proud when he told her that he had recited a sonnet in less than fourteen seconds: a second a line. His father, equally understandably, asked him what the poem meant. Rosenfeld replied that he'd never said it slowly enough to know: his father would have to ask one of the girls. Rosenfeld's prowess, he tells us, has been used many times since to impress people at parties. I can see its social value now as I write. As a way of learning about Shakespeare it has a certain serious deficiency of – let's call it 'civilisation', and will stand here for other less extreme examples of rote learning.

So I disagree with my correspondents who think children should learn by rote. I have two questions about children today learning Shakespeare's words: Why should they do it? I have demonstrated above my own commitment to the private internalisation of loved lines. I wanted to do it. Children need to be helped in by heart memorising if they can gain some pleasure from it. I feel that the children quoted throughout this book had much pleasure in writing, and that this pleasure will supply the necessary motivation for by heart learning.

I feel supported in this view by the fact that none of the books that influenced me and my generation of teachers in the teaching of English in primary schools had any truck with rote learning. In Clegg, for example, Thompson notes how in the schools represented in that exemplary book 'Exercises and drills seem to be anathema' (1965: ix). There are no index references to 'rote learning' in the harbinger of linguistic creativity in schools, Hourd (1949), Whitehead (1966), Peel (1967) or in Thompson (1969). The subject is, of course, irrelevant in Brownjohn (1980, 1982, 1989), Corbett and Moses (1986) and Pirrie (1987) because these books are about children writing. But who could think of teachers in the classrooms described in these books making children learn by rote?

In the last few years we have gone backwards in thinking that rote learning has any educational (as opposed to training) function in schools at all. And if any reader should suggest that the list of books in the last paragraph is in some way representative of a sixties 'sentimentality', I would direct him or her to the quality of the writing in those books.

I offer one example in my earlier book (1997: 166–7) where a whole school learned the last song from *Twelfth Night* (V:1:388–407):

> The headteacher says the odd-numbered lines while the children to his left say the line 'With hey, ho, the wind and the rain' and those to his right say 'For the rain it raineth every day' – except in the last stanza, of course. Both the headteacher and the children emphasize the rhythm crudely, shouting rather than sighing 'heigh-ho' for example. The headteacher says his lines in a suggestive voice and with appropriate actions. He swaggers and then staggers slightly in the third stanza, and mimes tossing off a pint. There's the hint of a hangover in the fourth. If this is crude, the headteacher says another day they will discuss how the poem might be said differently, and then speak it more reflectively. On another they might listen to one of the many settings of the song.
>
> Subtly or not, the children say their lines (and listen to their friends' lines) with evident enjoyment, even though the poem, or song, is full of terms ('man's estate', 'knaves', 'wive', 'swaggering', 'thrive', 'tosspots' and 'all that's one') that mean nothing to them. Indeed, far from cutting difficulty out from the poems we read to children, we should combine it with our expressive reading and acting (the headteacher toping, slurring and swaggering, for example) to show them what words mean headteacher says the odd-numbered lines…

This headteacher saw the Trevor Nunn film of *Twelfth Night* shortly after this and found Ben Kingsley's singing and the setting of the song helpful in developing this work. There are examples of children writing in imitation of this song in my afterword.

Here, though, we have moved slyly from 'rote' back to 'heart'. The children are not learning these words because they have to, or because they have been ordered to, but because these words are being written on their hearts in this teaching. Or, more accurately, they are writing the words on their hearts themselves.

In 'Shakespeare in Schools', no. 21, there is a beautiful description by Alison Stowe of Year 4 children working with her on Enorbarbus's speech from *Antony and Cleopatra* 'The barge she sat in' (II:2:201–14). After various warm-up activities, Stowe gave each child a line or phrase from the speech:

...every child had to greet each other saying their words. We then jogged around shouting the line and then whispering it...[the children] re-enacted a scene from a launderette: folding clothes, checking for dirt, pouring in powder; just saying their own line or phrase....We put the whole scene together by seating the children in a circle and getting them to come to the centre and say their line as if to Cleopatra herself...we invited the class teacher to stand in the middle and each child came forward, spoke the line and made an appropriate gesture. [They] were then grouped as though watching the barge float past. As each spoke their line it was easy to imagine the queen being there...

('Shakespeare in Schools', no. 21, Summer 1993)

This became a model for my work with other speeches from Shakespeare's plays which I re-jigged in different ways for different circumstances. Part of the trick is to be minimalist about it. Each group of children learned one line or even half a line at first. Although, as the exercise went on, other lines not assigned to them seeped into their minds. Another part of the trick is to use speeches and songs with repeating lines.

The best examples of speeches in Shakespeare for by heart learning are those that pre-suppose experiences that the children are likely to have had. The children quoted on p. 119 spoke the words 'Fear no more' in unison and then said the other lines in small groups or individually. The deaths of pets that they had loved informed their reading of the poem, and, as can be clearly seen, their writing. It was likely too, of course, that some of the children had experienced grief following the deaths of grandparents, parents and even siblings. Similarly, the children who learned 'I'll follow you' so readily were telling us (if we were attentive enough) something about playground life. What the children who learned the Porter's speech so well are telling us I am not sure.

Hughes has a startlingly different manner of learning by heart (1997). It is primarily visual: connect anything that you are trying to learn with a picture and find a way to connect the consecutive pictures with each other. The interested reader is directed to the introduction of his anthology. What follows here is an application of this method to the first few lines of a speech from *Antony and Cleopatra*:

> The barge she sat in, like a burnished throne
> Burned on the water. The poop was beaten gold;
> Purple the sails, and so perfumed that
> The winds were lovesick with them.

The Hughes method would be something like this: construct a series of images as follows:

a barge (a river vessel) with a woman sitting in it…
her seat is a large golden seat that is on fire, the flames…
coming up from a river over which we can see…
a high deck hammered till it is gold
purple sails, purple with bruising, hiding the high gold deck…

Hughes comments that 'if each image is "photographed" mentally…it will not be forgotten easily'. I find that this does not suit me. I do not see poetry in visual images as much as hear it and taste it. One of my correspondents said that, to her, it was about incantation and mantras: the sounds not the pictures mattered. 'I still can't walk across Westminster Bridge without saying to myself "Earth has not anything to show more fair…."' I feel the same. I cannot see my favourite poems in Hughes' terms; hardly at all. I have tried it with 'Love bade me welcome: yet my soul drew back,/Guiltie of dust and sin' by George Herbert and I found myself utterly seduced again by the sense of taste (the feel of the words in my mouth), my sense of hearing and my appreciation or version (changing subtly each time) of the meaning of the poem. The visual sense only came into the issue as I recalled how I saw the poem on the page. (But that is not quite true. Had I not always imagined Love's 'quick' eyes, and the clean white cloth on the table in 'You must sit down, sayes Love, and taste my meat…'.) I came across a more specific problem with the word 'perfumed' in the *Antony and Cleopatra* passage. I could not construct a visual image for it that did not seem absurd.

The children in this next example are learning more conventionally. They have been told the basics of the Ophelia plot in *Hamlet*. The contrast of this bare account with the rich detail of the speech served in itself to heighten children's awareness of what Gertrude is saying. They have looked at Millais' picture of Ophelia drowning and a bizarre photograph of Olivier directing Jean Simmons in this scene for his film (see Aers and Wheale). I then read Gertrude's account of Ophelia's death. We divided it up like this:

There is a willow/grows aslant a brook,/
That shows his hoar leaves/in the glassy stream./
Therewith fantastic garlands/did she make,/
Of crow-flowers,/nettles, daisies,/and long purples,/
That liberal shepherds/give a grosser name,/
But our cold maids/do dead men's fingers call them./
There on the pendant boughs/her cronet weeds/
Clamb'ring to hang,…/an envious sliver broke,/
When down her weedy trophies/and herself/
Fell in the weeping brook./Her clothes spread wide,/
And mermaid-like/awhile they bore her up,/
Which time she chanted/snatches of old lauds/
As one incapable/of her own distress,/

Or like a creature/native and indued/
Unto that element./But long it could not be/
Till that her garments,/heavy with their drink,/
Pulled the poor wretch/from her melodious lay/
To muddy death.

(IV:7:166–82)

We wrote each phrase, clause or sentence on separate cards which we numbered. 'There is a willow' was number one, 'grows aslant a brook' number two, and so on. We gave the cards out and said the poem a couple of times until the words became familiar. Then I asked the children to say the speech as though the speaker was describing the death of someone she loved; of someone to whom she was indifferent; of someone about whom she felt some guilt. I asked the children to read the speech again: bitterly; angrily; sourly. Then again as to the dead person's boyfriend, brother or parents; or as to a stranger such as a newspaper reporter; or to a television camera. Then we swapped the cards around so that everyone had a different half-line and went through the process again. We did this until we felt we were running out of steam.

This took a long time. The children became deeply engaged in the activity. Then, taking a hint from Hughes, I asked the children to choose one of the phrases and to draw it. This way of learning can, obviously, be applied to other speeches, such as Mercutio's Queen Mab speech in I:4 of *Romeo and Juliet*. For an account of writing in the grip of this, see p. 113.

All the following speeches turned out to be ideal for this kind of activity:

King Lear	III:2:1–7	'Blow, winds, and crack your cheeks!'
Macbeth	IV:1:1–38	'Thrice the brindled cat...'
	II:1:43–58	'I am that merry wanderer of the night'
	III:1:87–94	'I'll follow you'
	III:2:137–44	'O Helen, goddess, nymph...'
A Midsummer Night's Dream	V:1:349	'Now the hungry lion roars'
Richard II	III:3:147–55	'I'll give my jewels...'
Romeo and Juliet	I:1:167–73	'O brawling love...'
	I:4:53–93	'O then I see Queen Mab hath been with you...'
The Tempest	I:2:396–403	'Full fathom five thy father lies'
	III:2:130–38	'Be not afeared, the isle is full of noises'

On one occasion, I gave children copies of Lamb's admirable *The Wordsworth Dictionary of Shakespeare Quotations* (1992) and asked them to find one or two lines they liked, and to commit them to memory. On the next day, I asked them what their lines meant. Janine, ten years old, had chosen Charmian's line to the soothsayer 'I love long life better than figs' from *Antony and Cleopatra* (I:2). She said it to the class in different ways emphasising different words and being triumphant, sarcastic and bitter by turns much as she had been taught to do with other speeches she'd used for inspiration in her writing. She explained that, much as she liked rich food, Charmian wanted to live for a long time much more. Then I asked her to look the line up in the play, put her chosen line in its context and say all the lines. On the next day, she came in having learnt this speech by heart. What her family thought of her intoning this in order to commit it to memory is not recorded:

> Let me be married to three kings in a forenoon and widow them all. Let me have a child at fifty, to whom Herod of Jewry may do homage. Find me to marry me with Octavius Caesar, and companion me with my mistress...

A boy had chosen the following line from *Henry IV Part 1*, where Mistress Quickly says to Falstaff 'You owe me money, Sir John; and now you pick a quarrel to beguile me of it' (3:3:40–67). There was no problem with the meaning here, and Mark and another boy put the line in the context of the quarrel between the two characters. After half an hour's private rehearsal, they acted the scene to the whole class.

All these are examples of children learning with a point to that learning that the children could readily understand. This is a long way from the parrot activities with which I started this chapter.

And now I am going to put learning Shakespeare more explicitly in the wider context of education, and education itself in the even wider context of what we are when we are human beings at our fullest and richest – what we are when we have faith and hope in ourselves, each other and our materials, and are able to live worshipping, not money, but love.

Chapter 8

Faith, hope, love and teaching

Three words – faith, hope and love – stand here as protest against ways of thinking and writing about education which have become domineering over the past twenty years (I mistyped 'tears' there and was tempted to leave it). As I write successive drafts (June, July, September 1998) mechanistic thinkers, 'dressed in a little brief authority', seem to be garnering ever greater powers much as leaders of ex-public utilities garner profits. In the latter case, the consumers – Yorkshire Water's, perhaps – look on incredulously. In the former, the teachers stare in depressed disbelief. Pronouncements almost day by day suggest that everyone controlling the teachers and the children in schools – OFSTED chiefs, inspectors, politicians, advisers – believe that the essence of what they call 'good practice' is enshrined in management and accountability. They do not understand that 'there's beggary in the love that can be reckoned'. They have faith, in fact, in nothing that can't be counted, put into a checklist and made cost-effective.

It is important to note that this accountability is not professional. It is not an accountability to colleagues and clients, but to those in charge. Teachers and children are caught at a powerless place in a loop that begins and ends with mandarins. The dominant way of looking at schooling suggests that the teacher who is capable of, and compliant enough for, that 'good practice' is the one to be treated as an exemplar. Indeed, such teachers are wheeled out in conferences about the literacy strategy, or setting, or specialist teaching, or whatever the latest fad is ('It worked for me'). I think that the teacher is merely a hired hand in the cold grip of his or her superiors: an uncomfortable position that is liable to lead to the loss of blood flow if not worse (it certainly is not a professional position).

The powers that be suggest that we can measure effective teaching through the medium of test results and league tables. Fashionable thinking is about attainment and standards, rather than learning. Both children and teachers have been imprisoned in structures made of words that are not educational but managerial. We can judge the current hegemony by its words, and the following will serve here as an instructive example. This is documentation from the 'Literacy and Numeracy National Project', specifically the paper dated 1

October 1997. As you read it, bear in mind the words of Shakespeare that have preceded these words throughout this book and the words of children writing under the influence of Shakespeare. Remember the rhythms and vigour of those words and their capacity to surprise, delight and horrify; to teach us and to set us free in an exploration of our own natures and everyone else's: 'the almost silent stream/that trickles over stones and pebbles…'. Children have come close to their own local habitations and been able to give them names through their writing in this book following Shakespeare's examples. Compare and contrast: what is this writing doing?

> The NLP [National Literacy Project] aims to raise literacy standards in primary schools in line with national expectations and to meet the Government's targets by the year 2002 by:

- improving the school's management of literacy through target-setting linked to systematic planning, monitoring and evaluation by headteachers, senior staff and governors;
- setting clear expectations bench-marked in a term-by-term structure; and
- improving the quality of teaching through more focused literacy instruction and effective classroom management…

> All classes must teach literacy for one hour per day of continuous, dedicated time.…Teachers (*sic*) resource books with 'banks' of ideas and suggestions are also being developed.…The strategy for implementation is a 'cascade' model so every link in the chain needs to be as robust as possible…

This language speaks volumes about the project's priorities. First, that initial clause begs the question: what if national expectations are not high enough? If we judged such expectations by the quality of the newspapers that most people read or the standard of political utterance, they are dismal indeed. Surely many children, through their play with words, transcend such blandly expressed aims and write better than most journalists are allowed to. They speak with more frankness than any politician would risk. Many of them are represented in this book and in my *Read My Mind* (Sedgwick 1997) and other books on children writing poetry: Langdon (1961), Clegg (1965), Brownjohn (1980, 1982, 1989), Corbett and Moses (1986), Pirrie (1987), Hull (1988), Cotton (1989) and Carter (1997). In the face of almost any single poem in these books, such aims are steamrollers flattening flowers.

Second, all the evaluation is to be done by managers of various kinds. The teachers themselves (except, presumably, deputy heads) have no say. The 'cascade' model (a glorious mixed metaphor introduced as the high point of the text) will ensure that all the teachers will receive are random drops of water. Worse, only cursory mention is made of the quality of the processes which children go through. Teachers are ordered to concentrate instead on the targets that children must achieve. Thus children are never valued or even considered for what they are in their daily here and now. Their only presence, and it is shadowy, is what they will be soon (if they achieve what is vaguely called 'national expectations') or won't be (if they don't). The notion of the literacy hour itself flies in the face of the fact that you cannot speak, listen or write in any lesson without using skills that the project would call literacy skills. Are we not being literate when we read a History or Geography textbook? Do we not talk to some purpose when we work together on a model or display? Does not music obviously, with its necessary attention to detail, support what is called 'literacy skills'?

'...setting clear expectations bench-marked in a term-by-term structure...improving the quality of teaching through more focused literacy instruction and effective classroom management...' Writers dealing with human beings like this are like trained motor mechanics operating on a live horse (Ellis 1991). I think it must be difficult to be seduced by this language and yet retain a sense of the power of Shakespeare's language and even, come to that, of the children's language. This committee English can only be drafted by writers who 'deny the unique character of every utterance'; who use a 'pasteurized English...in which all the dangerous bacteria that might start an irrelevant, intellectual ferment have been...killed off' (both quotations are from Flower 1966). And this is a central problem for any teacher. She has to split her mind in two: part of her mind has to read the dead words of mandarins and work out ways of making sense of those words – first in her silent thinking going home in the car or lying awake in bed at night; second in her planning, individually and in groups, and then, third, in the classroom. Meanwhile the other part of her mind is alert to the vigour, rhythm and pace of the words of poetry – in this case Shakespeare's and her children's. It is not only overwork and clerical detail that causes stress among teachers. It is coping with grandeur, truth and wisdom on the one hand and rubbish on the other – almost simultaneously, and fantasising a sentence in all this dross that is a mandarin owning up: 'though it be not written down, yet forget not that I am an ass'.

In contrast to the language of inspectors, advisers and politicians, I want to suggest that there are three very different components to the teaching of any subject well, and the language that we must use to think and write about it. These components are specially important in the teaching of Shakespeare. They are couched in language that the teacher whose mind is oriented both towards the language of Shakespeare and, even more importantly, to the language of children will readily comprehend without wringing her mind painfully in two. St Paul was ahead of me by two millennia when he wrote: 'And now abideth faith, hope, charity[1], these three; but the greatest of these is charity' (I Corinthians 13:13).

1   Meaning love

I am aware that faith, hope and love will look today, among all that control-ling mechanism, like Miranda, Perdita and Imogen among the male schemers who would trap them, or (probably a more dangerous and certainly a less inter-esting situation) like free spirits in a behaviourist psychologist's testing room. But I have to stand by what I believe in – the centrality of faith, hope and love to what we are when we honestly teach. Watching teachers in classrooms where the children are engaged, I notice these three components. I see faith and hope first of all, and most importantly, in the teachers' view of the children whatever they are doing. These teachers expect and believe that the children's under-standing will be deepened by the lesson, and, that if it is not, it won't be the fault of the children. If we have faith and hope in the child, we will have high expectations of what he or she can do. The children quoted in this book have immeasurably increased my expectations of what the children I meet in the future will achieve.

There is, in contrast, a conventional view of teaching which I have called elsewhere (Sedgwick 1999) a 'deficit' model. I will call it here a faithless/hope-less model. People who have this view of teaching – whether they are teachers or administrators, parents or politicians – see children as they wait in the class-room as essentially lacking in something. We think in terms of this model when we say about a child's reading 'she hasn't begun at all', despite the fact that she can read public signs readily and rapidly; when we say to a visiting writer 'You won't get much out of him, he isn't creative' or 'This Year 5 is a poor lot'. If we believe in this model, we will transmit information to children without our understanding, first, that they already have much knowledge, and, second, that education is, at a basic level, about relating the new information to the infor-mation that they already have.

We need to have faith and hope, as well, in what we are teaching. This can be seen clearly in classrooms where a teacher has an almost palpable passion for what she is doing. Here we are concerned with children writing in the light of Shakespeare's model, and we need to believe that model is accessible and rele-vant to the child's needs. We need to have faith in Shakespeare's words rather than merely the stories he uses. I am always impressed when reading, acting or hamming up Shakespeare's lines to children by how much, first, children know and understand ideas that I did not dream they would know and understand; and, second, by how much they can infer of what they don't know from what they do already know; and, third, by how much effort they are able and willing to put into new understanding of words that are conventionally thought of as difficult. Children do not, as the actor Rex Harrison did, shrug Shakespeare off or patronize him: 'I know he's a great playwright and all that, and I shouldn't be saying this, but I do find him very difficult to understand, let alone play' (Lamb 1992: 343).

We need to have faith in Shakespeare's extraordinary ability to challenge and motivate the imaginations of all who come into lively contact with him; who can get beyond his egregious and infinitely problematical greatness, the sheer nuisance of his cultural status as the Bard of Avon, and let their minds wander faithfully, hopefully and with love in his mind's grasp.

Above all, it seems to me, we have to work as a profession to restore our faith and our hope in ourselves, both as individuals and as groups working together to discuss ways of making our teachering better: more creative, more inspiring, more truthful and less sentimental, less compliant, less cowed. We can do this in the light of the fact that we know what we are doing when we teach, and those who would cow us do not. I do not say this is going to be easy. As I write, the language is depressing still. I only have to pick up a newspaper to read about statistics that show that schools are still deemed to be 'failing', that teachers are leaving because they can't stand the stress. I know that short lists for deputy headships are the same, more or less, as the long lists. Partly (I hope) because few teachers want to manage the systematic vilification of a profession any further.

So now abideth faith and hope. The greatest component of good teaching is love: love for the child, love for the plays and poems of Shakespeare and love for the teaching that links the two in such a potent union. (I once saw an infant headteacher hug and kiss a child. I want to say clearly that I don't mean that kind of love. I am sure that the child wasn't at any risk of abuse. But I did feel that he wasn't being sufficiently respected by his headteacher.) I mean by love that attempt at an 'absolutely pure attention' that Weil talks about (Panichas 1977: 18). For Paul, of course, that love (here translated as 'charity')

> ...suffereth long, and is kind;...envieth not; vaunteth not itself, is not puffed up, doth not behave itself unseemly, seeketh not her own, is not easily provoked, thinketh no evil; rejoiceth not in iniquity, but rejoiceth in the truth; beareth all things, believeth all things, hopeth all things, endureth all things...

and we may or may not think these attributes are suitable for a teacher.

I would say that love in a teacher shows itself in the contact of ear and eye with the child. A contact that is unremitting while that child needs it; in a concentration on the child's writing, or picture, or maths or science or whatever. This concentration is given for higher motives than success in test results and position in league tables. It is given because it will deepen the child's understanding. The things that the teacher rejoices in, bears, believes in, hopes for and endures are what the children can do and will do given a proper faith and hope in those children and in the light that shines inside them. This love will enable the children to set themselves a glass where they might see not only themselves and their darkest parts ('I'm small, the world's big...'), but their brightness, too; the world around them ('various libraries for knowledge/As I grow the libraries get bigger...'); and will help them to see each piece of writing as a little research project between themselves and the rest of their world.

Afterword

The wind and the rain

At the end of *Twelfth Night*, the clown appears and sings his famous song, 'The Wind and the Rain', ending with the words 'But that's all one, our play is done' (V:1:366–85). Children love this song, especially as sung by Ben Kingsley (see References for details). The last task I set children while writing this book was to imitate this poem and what they wrote serves as an epilogue or an afterword. As they composed these verses, they reflected on life and death in many of its glories and sadnesses, as all the children had in the writing in this book. They played cheerfully with the tricks of language, especially rhythm and repetition. They delighted in pleasure and obscurity, free from the pressures of the literacy hour; clowning around, instead, in real life:

> When I was just a baby in a cot
> with the snakes and spiders all around
> I played with the dog and I played with the cat
> with the snakes and spiders all around
>
> When I left to Borough Estate
> with the snakes and spiders all around
> I was the centre of all attention
> with the snakes and spiders all around
>
> When sixty or more I lost my hair
> with the snakes and spiders all around
> then I was skull and bones underground
> with the snakes and spiders all around
>
> (Adam, 9)

Melissa, eleven years old, wrote her song in a hurry while listening to Ben Kingsley singing, and it can be the last word in the book – apart from the administrative data of appendices: practical notes, lesson plans, references, index and other useful (I trust) but unliterary, unchildlike lists.

When I was a lass in the garden of the green
CHORUS From hurricanes to winds decrease
I used to live but all myself
CHORUS Come to rain and wind all around.

And when I grew I knew to fly
CHORUS From hurricanes to winds decrease
I loved to live with a piggle-doodle-die
CHORUS Come to rain and wind all around.

And then I grew up to be huge
CHORUS From hurricanes to winds decrease
I loved the world and all its living
CHORUS Come to rain and wind all around.

Just live in justice and Catholic priests
CHORUS From hurricanes to winds decrease
I think that life is better than death
CHORUS Come to rain and wind all around.

Appendix

A practical note about lesson plans and other issues

One of the readers of a typescript of this book suggested that I supplied 'lesson plans' for each of the case studies. I have not done this for two reasons. First, I think that teachers are able to work out their own plans. The profession has many problems these days and one of them is composed of the thousands of omnipotent, intellectual and creative individuals and organisations – politicians, inspectors, advisers, academics, publishers, journalists, writers – who conspire to tell teachers both what to do and how to do it with varying degrees of tact and grace. Teachers' status has been reduced, largely, to that of hired hands. In contrast, I would rather offer much passion and a little knowledge about a subject (in this case Shakespeare) on the unfashionable assumption that teachers can, do and should think for themselves; can, do and should reflect on the subject they are teaching and its relationship to the children in their classes. That, to take this a stage further, they can collaborate with each other to improve standards in classrooms without the dubious benefit of the crasser forms of managerialism with which we are all now afflicted.

It follows from this, for me, that teachers are active learners too. Books about teaching are essentially books that enable teachers to think further and more deeply about their practice, rather than books that tell them what to think.

Second, all the lessons follow (for me) roughly the same pattern: I read the passage to the children as carefully as I can. If it is one (this was not uncommon) that I am not familiar with, I practise it the night before. I try to put as much expression into my reading as possible without distorting the meaning. Then, I say it again, explaining any problems of meaning (usually with the help of Rex Gibson's Cambridge Schools Shakespeare) and changing the mode of expression. Then the children and I (and sometimes other adults present: teacher, nursery nurse, classroom helper, parent) *play* with the passage. I say it phrase by phrase and they say it after me, imitating my manner of saying it. I vary my delivery. For example, I might say Puck's speech at III:1:87, beginning by whispering the first few phrases, then getting louder and louder and then growing quieter again. Also, I might say the speech and get the children in groups to repeat each phrase or miss out words which they have to say. Sometimes, one of the children will lead the class in saying the speech in one of these ways. Fellow-teachers will have no difficulty thinking of other ways of playing with Shakespeare's words.

Then, typically, I have a period of intense silence, because 'our creative depth is the depth in which we are quiet' (Tillich 1962: 108). The children 'have to be attentive to what is about to happen....We must...let the Holy Ghost, or the Muse, or the subconscious – if you prefer modern mythology – have its way with us...' (Jorge Luis Borges quoted in McShane 1973: 149ff.). Once I am fairly sure that the play and silence have done their important work, I ask the children to write – the results of which I have printed throughout this book. I constantly emphasize that the children are writing first drafts (see illustrations). This might be a good point to say a word about drafting as the most important among three standing orders for writing using the words of Shakespeare as a stimulus:

Standing Order No. 1: Writing takes more than one draft. The second draft should be just that: a post on the road home, a very temporary stay against confusion, not home itself, not, please not a beautiful piece of italic script prepared for the wall or the child's file with its air of finality. It should be scribbled on as new ideas come and old ones are discarded. Lines should signify the addition of new ideas and words.

This is all to say that children must be freed from the despotism of the fair copy. Nobody ever completes writing anything they think of as important – a love letter, a poem, an application for a job, a story, a request for a bank loan – without going through at least two drafts first. In the same way, children should not start writing their poems inspired by Shakespeare with a piece of paper that they think is the only one they'll have; that, if they make a mistake, whether trivial (spelling, punctuation, handwriting) or major (content), they have thereby ruined the whole thing. It is probably best to work on large pieces of cheap paper with a pencil that has been trained not to mind crossing out, scribbling in margins and even doodling.

Children should not use erasers, because first they are excuses for wasting time, second because children might rub out something good that they'll want back, but thirdly, and much more importantly, they speak of wrong reasons for writing. We are not writing to make nice marks on paper, but to continue the old search for the truth that each new generation, and each new writer in each generation, however young, is engaged in. Why else write?

Standing Order No. 2: In Ezra Pound's words, make it new. While life can cope with repetition and cliché, art cannot. An acquaintance once read some new poems in a magazine, and said he thought them a 'bit harsh – where are the "verdant pastures"'? The verdant pastures weren't there, of course, because they have already been used – in a hymn version of the 23rd Psalm. The problem for the writer in any generation can be summed up crudely like this: how do you

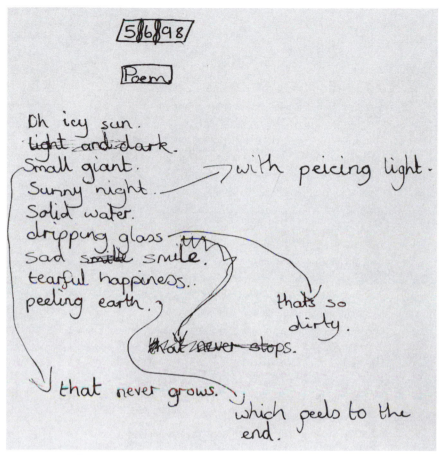

Illustration 4 Draft (Anon)

look at green fields where lambs might graze, be struck by their beauty and write about them in a new way?

Children have to listen to and read Shakespeare's words, and then make something of them that while lit and nourished by Shakespeare, is, nevertheless, not Shakespeare. I sometimes tell children that 'Alan will think of things that Mandy won't think of. Amber will get ideas that Daniel won't get…' and so on. When a child contributes something fresh to the discussion before writing, I often suggest that he or she writes it down: 'That's good – and it's yours – nobody else can have that. Write it down before you forget it'. Often children riding their luck can produce utterly new sentences and they should be taught to value this luck: 'What have we done to deserve depth', for example, was written during my lesson on the opening of *The Tempest* (p. 66).

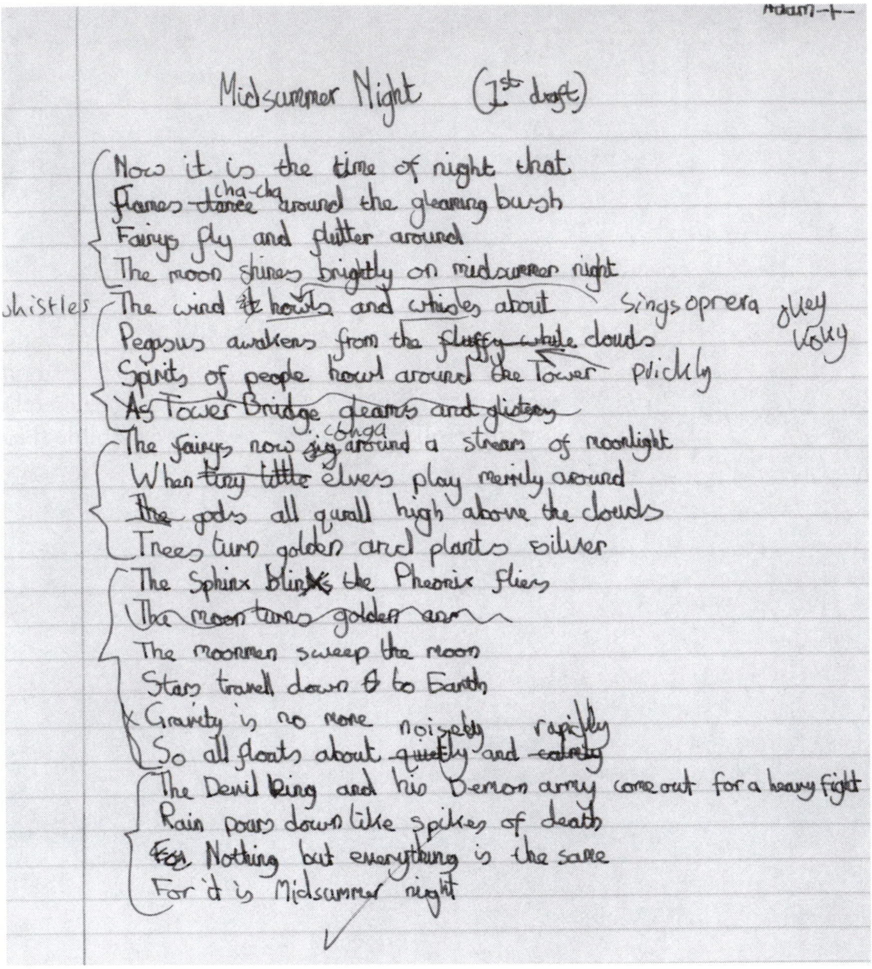

Adam

Midsummer Night (1st draft)

Now it is the time of night that
Flames ~~dance~~ cha-cha around the gleaming bush
Fairys fly and flutter around
The moon shines brightly on midsummer night
whistles The wind howls and whistles about Sings oprera
Pegasus awakens from the fluffy white clouds
Spirits of people howl around the Tower prickly
~~As Tower Bridge gleams and glisteny~~
The fairys now ~~jig~~ conga around a stream of moonlight
When ~~tiny little~~ elves play merrily around
~~The~~ gods all quall high above the clouds
Trees turn golden and plants silver
The Sphinx blinks the Pheonix fliers
~~The moon turns golden an~~
The moonmen sweep the moon
Stars travell down to Earth
Gravity is no more noisely rapidly
So all floats about ~~quietly~~ and ~~calmly~~
The Devil king and his Demon army come out for a heavy fight
Rain pours down like spikes of death
~~For~~ Nothing but everything is the same
For it is Midsummer night

Illustration 5 First draft: Adam (11)

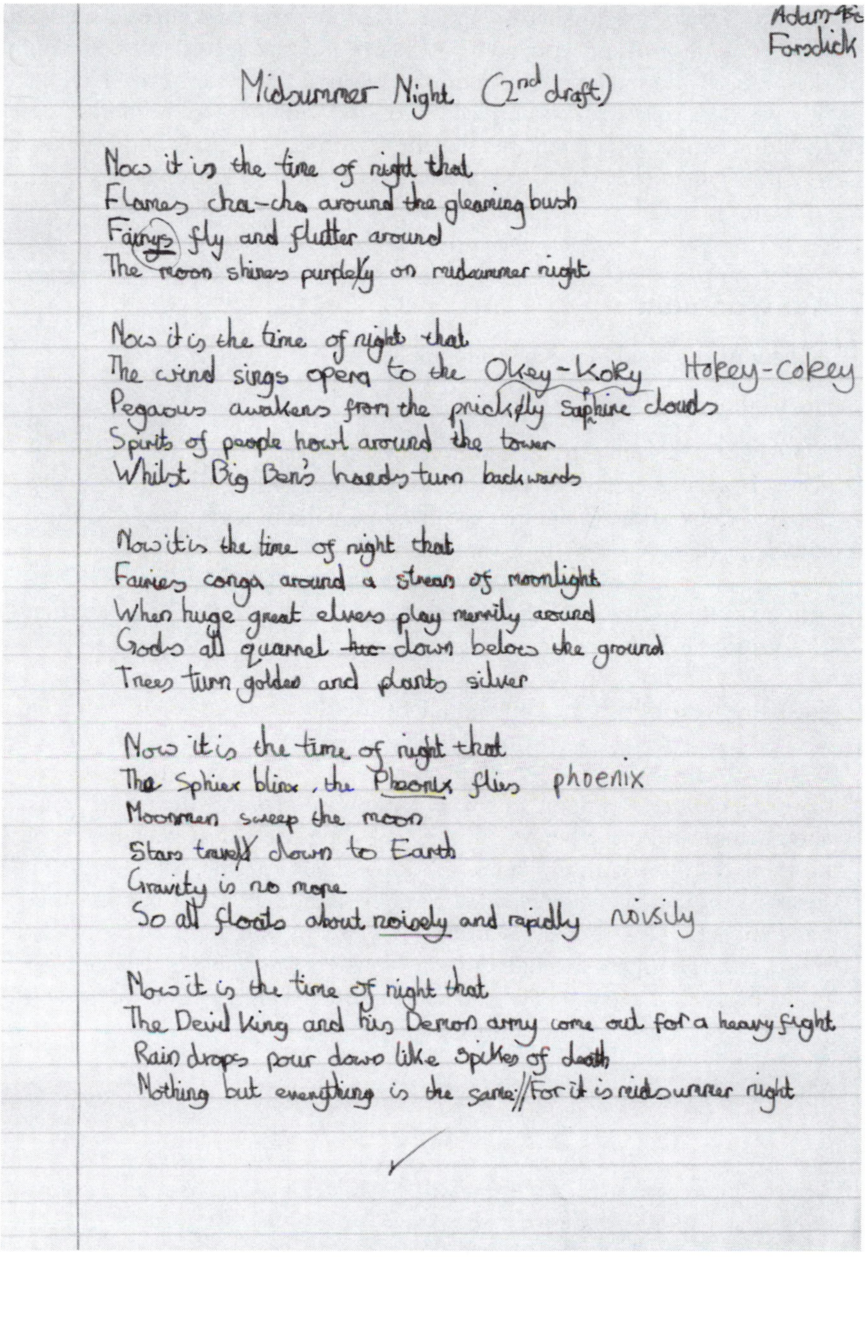

Adam
Forsdick

Midsummer Night (2nd draft)

Now it is the time of night that
Flames cha-cha around the gleaming bush
Fairys fly and flutter around
The moon shines purplely on midsummer night

Now it is the time of night that
The wind sings opera to the Okey-Koky   Hokey-cokey
Pegasus awakens from the prickerly Saphire clouds
Spirits of people howl around the tower
Whilst Big Ben's hands turn backwards

Now it is the time of night that
Fairies conga around a stream of moonlight
When huge great elves play merrily around
Gods all quarrel too down below the ground
Trees turn golden and plants silver

Now it is the time of night that
The Sphinx blinx, the Phoenix flies   phoenix
Moonmen sweep the moon
Stars travel down to Earth
Gravity is no more
So all floats about noisely and rapidly   noisily

Now it is the time of night that
The Devil King and his Demon army come out for a heavy fight
Rain drops pour down like spikes of death
Nothing but everything is the same//For it is midsummer night

Illustration 6 Second draft: Adam (11)

Standing Order No. 3: There is more than one way to compose. Children should get used to writing with word processors and tape recorders as, no doubt, Shakespeare would have done had they been available in his day. This helps greatly with drafting: writers can place lines and sentences in a different order so that they strike up different relationships with one another and often send new sparks flying. They can also eliminate coarseness and repetitions with the tap of a finger.

A lesson plan

A lesson plan would look something like this:

Aims of this lesson: Children will use Shakespeare's words to learn (a) about themselves and (b) about the words by composing the first draft of a new piece of writing. (I aim that the children will enjoy the words, so there will be no element of anything that might resemble 'drill'.)

Introduction: Familiarize the children with the chosen passage from Shakespeare in as many ways as possible.

Suggest ways in which the children might use the words to begin their own poems.

Give the children a minute or two of intense silence in which they think about this while composing phrases in their heads. Remember poor Posthumus in prison in *Cymbeline* thinking about his wife: 'O Imogen! I'll speak to thee in silence (V:4). When their hands shoot up because they have thought of a phrase, increase the burden: you want two phrases; three; four. The more Posthumus thought, the more Imogen became clear in his head. The more silence you can help the children find, the greater the quality of what they will think of and, later, produce.

The class listens to some of the phrases, and comments on each others' ideas.

The children write. This writing will be interrupted by plenary sessions when the children share what they have written and help each other to edit drafts. During the final plenary, children will read, in as polished a way as possible, their drafts. This session will be an evaluation as well, as everybody can begin to judge the quality of the teaching, learning and the poems written.

A list of parts of plays used in this book

I have only listed parts of plays where I have given pieces of children's writing, not passages I have suggested without examples. The page numbers refer to where the speech and the children's writing are.

Antony and Cleopatra III:13:20–1 'He wears the rose/Of youth upon him' (pp. 25ff.)

As You Like It I:2: 85–6 'With his mouth full of news' (pp. 22ff.)

I:3:36 'With his eyes full of anger' (pp. 22ff.)

II:7:12 ff. 'A fool, a fool!' (pp. 70ff.)

II:7:139–66 'All the world's a stage…' (pp. 73ff.)

A Comedy of Errors I:2 '…the meat is cold…' (pp. 30ff.)

II:2:194 'Thou drone, thou snail, thou slug, thou sot' (p. 83)

III:1:32 'Mome, malthouse, capon, coxcomb, idiot, patch!' (p. 83)

Coriolanus I:1:169–73 'He that trusts to you…' (p. 83)

Cymbeline IV:2:113–15 'This Cloten was a fool…' (p. 123)

IV:2:268–75 'Fear no more the heat o' the sun' (pp. 119ff.)

Hamlet III:4:19–20 'You go not till I set you up a glass…' (pp. xiii–xiv)

Henry IV Part 1 I:2:1–9 'Thou art so fat-witted' (pp. 80ff.)

II:3:7 'Out of this nettle, danger, we pluck this flower, safety' (p. 30)

IV: V:3:32 'I am as hot as molten lead, and as heavy too' (pp. 26ff.)

Henry IV Part 2 III:1:31 'Uneasy lies the head that wears a crown' (p. 30)

Henry V III:1 'Once more unto the breach…' (pp. 32ff.)

Julius Caesar IV:1:28–9 '– He is a tried and valiant soldier./–So is my horse' (p. 84)

King Lear III:2:1–7 'Blow, winds, and crack your cheeks!' (pp. 115ff.)

Macbeth I:1; I:3 'When the battle's lost, and won'; 'So foul and fair a day…'; 'Lesser than Macbeth, and stronger' (pp. 98ff.)

II:3 'Here's a knocking indeed…' (pp. 93ff.)

II:3:70 'Awake! Awake!' (pp. 97ff.)

IV:1:1–38 'Thrice the brindled cat…' (pp. 101ff.)

V:1 'What is it she does now?' (pp. 105ff.)

A Midsummer Night's Dream I:1 'Four days will quickly steep themselves in night' (pp. 40ff.)

II:1:43–58 'I am that merry wanderer of the night' (pp. 45ff.)

II:2:9–30 'You spotted snakes…' (pp. 52ff.)

III:1:87–94 'I'll follow you' (pp. 46ff.)

III:2:137–44 'O Helen, goddess, nymph…' (pp. 57ff.)

V:1 'Now the hungry lion roars' (pp. 60ff.)

Richard II II:4:7–12: ''Tis thought the King is dead; we will not stay' (pp. 34ff.)

III:3:147–55: 'I'll give my jewels for a set of beads' (pp. 36ff.)

Richard III V:4:7 'A horse! A horse! My kingdom for a horse!' (p. 30)

Romeo and Juliet I:1:167–73 'O brawling love…' (pp. 108ff.)

I:4:53–93 'O then I see Queen Mab hath been with you...' (pp. 112ff.)

III:2:75 ''O serpent heart...' (pp. 105ff.)

The Taming of the Shrew III:2:41–60 'Why, Petruchio is come...' (pp. 86ff.)

IV:3:107–14 'Thou liest, thou thread, thou thimble...' (pp. 81ff.)

The Tempest I:1:54 'Mercy on us! –' (pp. 65ff.)

I:2:396–403 'Full fathom five thy father lies' (pp. 66ff.)

III:2:130–8 'Be not afeared, the isle is full of noises' (pp. 68ff.)

Titus Andronicus: II:1:58–9 'Foul-spoken coward, that thund'rest with thy tongue! (p. 85)

The Winter's Tale (I:2:426–7) '...you may as well/Forbid the sea for to obey the moon...' (pp. 27ff.)

I:2:8–30 'There was a man ...' (p. 29)

V:1:205 'The stars, I see, will kiss the valleys first' (pp. 27ff.)

A glossary for Biondello's speech about Petruchio's arrival at his own wedding, *The Taming of the Shrew* III:2:41–60.

jerkin	jacket
chapeless	without the metal covering that protects the point
hipped	with a dislocated hip
glanders	various diseases
mose in the chine	
lampass	
windgalls	
spavins	
yellows	
staggers	
the fives	
the bots	
sped	ruined
rayed	disfigured
begnawn	eaten away
shoulder-shotten	with dislocated shoulder
crupper	strap which passes under the horse's tail
pack-thread	string

The answers to the riddles on pp. 63–4: jazz, eye, Puck, dream, potion.

References

Lesley Aers and Nigel Wheale (1991) *Shakespeare in the Changing Curriculum*, London, Routledge

Kingsley Amis (1954) *Lucky Jim*, London, Gollancz

John Betjeman (1958) *Collected Poems*, London, John Murray

Michael Billington (1998) 'Exit, pursued by boos' in *Guardian*, 1 June

William Blake (1826) in *Oxford Dictionary of Quotations*, third edn, Oxford, Oxford University Press, 1979

Janet Bottoms (1994) 'Playing with Shakespeare: or "Where there's a will there's a way"' in *English in Education*, vol. 28, no. 3

Sandy Brownjohn (1980) *Does it Have to Rhyme?: Teaching Children to Write Poetry*, London, Hodder & Stoughton

Sandy Brownjohn (1982) *What Rhymes with 'Secret'?: Teaching Children to Write Poetry*, London, Hodder & Stoughton

Sandy Brownjohn (1989) *The Ability to Name Cats: Teaching Children to Write Poetry*, London, Hodder & Stoughton

A S Byatt (1979) *The Virgin in the Garden*, London, Chatto & Windus

H Caldwell Cook (1917) *The Play Way*, London, Heinemann

Roy Campbell (1930) *Adamastor*, London, Faber & Faber

Dennis Carter (1997) *The Power to Overwhelm: Comprehensive Approaches to Poetry in the Primary School*, Clwyd Poetry Project

Charles Causley (1970) *Figgie Hobbin*, London, Macmillan

Charles Causley (ed.) (1974) *The Puffin Book of Magic Verse*, London, Puffin

Charles Causley (1996) *Collected Poems for Children*, London, Macmillan

Alec Clegg (1964) *The Excitement of Writing*, London, Chatto & Windus

Samuel Taylor Coleridge in *Oxford Dictionary of Quotations*, third edn, Oxford, Oxford University Press, 1979

John Cotton (1992) *Here's Looking at You Kid*, North Wales and Wirral, Headland

John Cotton (1998) private letter

John Cotton and Fred Sedgwick (1996) *Two by Two*, Ipswich, Tricky Sam! Press

T Crehan (1965) *The Poetry of Wordsworth*, London, University of London Press

Bernard Crick (1982) *George Orwell: A Life*, London, Penguin

Kevin Crossley-Holland (1982) *The Riddle Book*, London, Macmillan

Charles Darwin in G F Lamb's *The Wordsworth Dictionary of Shakespeare Quotations*, Ware, Wordsworth, 1992

Emily Dickinson *The Complete Poems of Emily Dickinson*, ed. by Thomas H Johnson, London, Faber & Faber, 1970

Mary Jane Drummond (1993) *Assessing Children's Learning*, London, David Fulton

Alice Thomas Ellis (1991) *The Inn at the Edge of the World*, London, Penguin

T S Eliot (1963) *Collected Poems*, London, Faber & Faber

F D Flower (1966) *Language and Education*, London, Longmans

Leon Garfield (1997) *Shakespeare Stories*, London, Puffin Books

Rex Gibson (1987) in 'Shakespeare in Schools', no. 4, Cambridge, Cambridge Institute of Education

Rex Gibson (1990) in 'Shakespeare in Schools', no. 11, Cambridge, Cambridge Institute of Education

Rex Gibson (1993)'A black day will it be to somebody' in Morag Styles and Mary Jane Drummond *The Politics of Reading*, Cambridge, University of Cambridge and Homerton College

Rex Gibson (1998) *Teaching Shakespeare*, Cambridge, Cambridge University Press

Maurice Gilmour (ed.) (1997) 'Shakespeare for All' vol. 1: The Primary School, London, Cassell

Donald Graves (1983) *Writing: Teachers and Children at Work*, London, Heinemann

Ian Hamilton (1982) *Robert Lowell: A Biography*, London, Faber & Faber

Seamus Heaney (1966) *Death of a Naturalist*, London, Faber & Faber

Seamus Heaney (1984) *Station Island*, London, Faber & Faber

Wayne F Hill and Cynthia J Ottchen (1991) *Shakespeare's Insults: Educating Your Wit*, Cambridge, MainSail Press

Horace *The Complete Odes and Epodes with the Centennial Hymn*, trans. by W G Shepherd, London, Penguin, 1983

Horace *The Odes of Horace*, trans. by James Michie, London, Penguin, 1967

Marjorie L Hourd (1949) *The Education of the Poetic Spirit: A Study in Children's Expression in the English Lesson*, London, Heinemann

Geoffrey Hughes (1998) *Swearing: A Social History of Foul Language, Oaths and Profanity in English*, London, Penguin

Ted Hughes (ed.) (1991) *A Choice of Shakespeare's Poetry*, London, Faber & Faber

Ted Hughes (1992) *Shakespeare and the Goddess of Complete Being*, London, Faber & Faber

Ted Hughes (ed.) (1997) *By Heart: 101 Poems to Remember*, London, Faber & Faber

Robert Hull (1988) *Behind the Poem: A Teacher's View of Children Writing*, London, Routledge

Samuel Johnson in James Boswell (1906) *The Life of Samuel Johnson L.L.D Volume Two*, London, Dent

Jan Kott (1967) *Shakespeare our Contemporary*, London, Routledge

G F Lamb (1992) *The Wordsworth Dictionary of Shakespeare Quotations*, Ware, Wordsworth

Margaret Langdon (1961) *Let the Children Write – an Explanation of Intensive Writing*, London, Longman

Geraldine McCaughrean (1997) *Stories from Shakespeare*, London, Orion

Frank McShane 'Borges on poetry' in *Poetry Dimension* ed. by J Robson, London, Abacus, 1973

Martial *The Epigrams*, selected and translated by James Michie, London, Penguin, 1978

Martial translated by Porter: see Porter

Priscilla Meyer (1988) *Find What the Sailor has Hidden: Vladimir Nabokov's Pale Fire*, Connecticut, Wesleyan University Press

Arthur Miller (1987) *Timebends: A Life*, London, Methuen

John Mole and Mary Norman (1979) *Once There were Dragon: A Book of Riddles in Words and Pictures*, London, Deutsch

Vladimir Nabokov (1992) *Pale Fire*, London, Everyman

A S Neill (1969) *Summerhill*, London, Penguin

Iona and Peter Opie (1973) *The Oxford Book of Children's Verse*, London, Oxford University Press

George Panichas (1977) *The Simone Weil Reader*, New York, David MacKay

Brian Patten (ed.) (1991) *The Puffin Book of Twentieth-Century Children's Verse* London, Viking

Eric Partridge (1948) *Shakespeare's Bawdy*, London, Routledge

Philippa Pearce (1992) 'The making of stories for children' in Styles, Bearne and Watson *After Alice*, London, Cassell

Marie Peel (1971) *Seeing to the Heart: English and Imagination in the Junior School*, London, Chatto & Windus

Jill Pirrie (1987) *On Common Ground: A Programme for Teaching Poetry*, London, Hodder & Stoughton

Sylvia Plath (1981) *Collected Poems*, London, Faber & Faber

Peter Porter (1972) *After Martial*, Oxford, Oxford University Press

Emily Roeves (unpublished) versions of the epigrams of Martial

Mordecai Rosenfeld (1998) 'On first learning Shakespeare as a boy in Brooklyn' in *Poetry Nation Review*, vol. 25, no. 5

Delphine Ruston (1998) private letter

Vernon Scannell (1987) quoted in *Teaching Poetry in the Secondary School*, London, HMSO

Fred Sedgwick (1994) *Personal, Social and Moral Education*, London, David Fulton

Fred Sedgwick (1997) *Read my Mind: Young Children, Poetry and Learning*, London, Routledge

Fred Sedgwick (1999) *Thinking about Literacy: Young Children and their Language*, London, Routledge

Martin Seymour-Smith (1975) *Sex and Society*, London, Hodder & Stoughton

George Bernard Shaw (1907) in *Oxford Dictionary of Quotations*, third edn, Oxford, Oxford University Press, 1979

Shakespeare in Schools (1987) no. 4, Cambridge, Cambridge University Institute of Education

Shakespeare in Schools (1993) no. 21, Cambridge, Cambridge University Institute of Education

Francis Stillman (1966) *The Poet's Manual and Rhyming Dictionary*, London, Thames and Hudson

Morag Styles, Eve Bearne and Victor Watson (eds) (1992) *After Alice: Exploring Children's Literature*, London, Cassell

Morag Styles and Mary Jane Drummond (1993) *The Politics of Reading*, Cambridge, University of Cambridge and Homerton College

Morag Styles (1998) *From the Garden to the Street: Three Hundred Years of Poetry for Children*, London, Cassell

Paul Theroux (1978) article in *Time*

Edward Thomas (1981)*The Collected Poems*, ed. by R George Thomas, Oxford, Oxford University Press

Denys Thompson (ed.) (1969) *Directions in the Teaching of English*, Cambridge, Cambridge University Press

Paul Tillich (1962) *The Shaking of the Foundations*, London, Penguin

Helen Vendler (1997) *The Art of Shakespeare's Sonnets*, Cambridge MA, Harvard University Press 1997

P E Vernon (ed.) (1970) *Creativity*, London, Penguin

Frank Whitehead (1966) *The Disappearing Dais: A Study of the Principles and Practice of English Teaching*, London, Chatto & Windus

Anthony Wilson (1998) *The Poetry Book for Primary Schools*, London, The Poetry Society

John Worthen (1991) *D H Lawrence: The Early Years 1885–1912*, Cambridge, Cambridge University Press

Two compact discs

The soundtrack of the film *Twelfth Night*, directed by Trevor Nunn, track 19: Ben Kingsley singing Shaun Davey's setting of 'The Wind and the Rain'. Silva Screen records Film CD 186

Bryn Terfel: *The Vagabond*, track 12: 'Fear no more the heat o' the sun'. Deutsche Grammophon 445 946 2

Editions of Shakespeare's plays and poems used

I recommend the Cambridge school editions of the plays – both for initial study and preparation, and for the pupils. The volumes are attractive, relatively cheap, and the assistance provided by the notes is tactful and handily placed opposite each side of the text. These notes contain helpful exercises which, if I were a teacher coming to the plays for the first time, I would find enlightening. The books are intended mostly for secondary schools, but any primary school serious about bringing Shakespeare into the ken of its children should have at least some copies of *A Midsummer Night's Dream*, *Macbeth*, *The Tempest*, *Romeo and Juliet* and *The Comedy of Errors*. The Oxford School Shakespeare also provides useful options. Unless otherwise stated, all editions are in the Cambridge School Shakespeare, General Editor Rex Gibson.

All's Well That Ends Well (Huddlestone and Innes 1993)
A Midsummer Night's Dream (Buckle and Kelley 1992)
Macbeth (Gibson 1993)
The Tempest (Gibson 1995)
Romeo and Juliet (Gibson 1992)
The Comedy of Errors (Andrews 1992)
King Lear (Bain, Morris and Smith 1996)
Antony and Cleopatra (Berry and Clamp 1990)
Hamlet (Gibson 1994)

I have also used:

As You Like It edited by Agnes Latham (1975) London, Methuen (The Arden Shakespeare)
Cymbeline edited by J M Noswothy (1955) London, Methuen (The Arden Shakespeare)
Henry IV Part 1 edited by Herbert Weil and Judith Weil (1997) Cambridge, Cambridge University Press
The Winter's Tale edited by J H P Pafford (1966) London, Methuen (The Arden Edition)
The Winter's Tale edited by Roma Gill (1996) Oxford, Oxford University Press
Hamlet edited by John Dover Wilson (1948) Cambridge, Cambridge University Press
The Taming of the Shrew edited by Roma Gill (1996) Oxford, Oxford University Press

I have not used Shakespeare's sonnets with children, but these poems are central for any teacher interested in getting close to the essence of Shakespeare's writing. I have used in my personal study the following editions of the sonnets:

The Art of Shakespeare's Sonnets edited by Helen Vendler (1997), Cambridge MA, Harvard University Press

The Sonnets edited by Rex Gibson (1997), Cambridge, Cambridge University Press

The Sonnets and a Lover's Complaint edited by John Kerrigan (1986), London, Penguin

The Sonnets edited by John Dover Wilson (1966), Cambridge, Cambridge University Press

Shakespeare's Sonnets edited by Katherine Duncan-Jones (1997), Walton-on-Thames, Nelson

Shakespeare's Sonnets edited by Martin Seymour-Smith (1963), Portmouth NH, Heinemann

Index

accountability in education 136
Adler, Joseph, American actor as Lear 115
Aers, Lesley 7
alliteration and assonance 49, 67, 102–3
Amis, Kingsley ('a brief manic flurry of obscene gestures') 15
Amleth (by Saxo Grammaticus; a precursor of *Hamlet*) 19
Armstrong, Louis ('West End Blues') 130
Arnold, Matthew, sonnet about Shakespeare 3
attention to children's poems, the necessity of 48
Auden, W H 42, 127

Baker, Janet 129
bawdy in Shakespeare, and children 6, 15–17, 56, 80
Bennett, Hywel 12
Betjemam, John and his use of brand names 101
Bible, The 53, 59, 69, 138–40
Billington, Michael 42
Blake, William 4
Bottoms, Janet 6
Bowdler, Thomas 16
Britton, Tony 12
Brownjohn, Sandy 42, 76
Butler, Samuel 42
Byatt, A S 7, 126

caesura (break in poetic line) 37
Caldwell Cook, H 1
Campbell, Roy 107
Carter, Cathy 21
Carter, Dennis 21–2
Causley, Charles 1, 102

Charles, Prince 6, 11, 59, 77
Coleridge, Samuel Taylor, on Shakespeare's difficulty 13
Coles, Jane 6
Connolly, Billy, and guilt 89
conscience and *Macbeth* 90
Cotton, John 2, 7, 11, 17

Darwin, Charles, view of Shakespeare 10
Dedalus, Stephen 89
Dickinson, Emily 7, 96
difficulty of Shakespeare 13
Douglas, I 21
drafting 144
Drummond, Mary Jane 80
Dunblane and *Macbeth* 90

editing friends – a technique for helping redraft 26, 53, 96, 139
expectations (teachers' of children, and their importance for learning) 26, 53, 96, 139

Finney, Albert 60
Finzi, Gerald, composer of setting of 'Fear no more' 121
Foreman, Michael 18
Freud, Sigmund 1, 12
friends, editing, *see* editing friends

Garfield, Leon, versions of Shakespeare 18
Gibson, Rex 13, 49, 51, 85–6, 89, 94, 143
Gilmour, Maurice 7–8, 17, 90, 94, 98
Globe Theatre, Sam Wannamaker's 17
Grammaticus, Saxo (author of Shakespeare's source for *Hamlet*) 19
Graves, Donald 20, 36

Graves, Robert 11
grecian-urning 10, 129
Greene, Robert (Shakespeare's
    contemporary, on 'that upstart crow')
    11

haiku 79
Harrison, Rex, on Shakespeare 139
Heaney, Seamus 7
Hell, and children thinking about it 89ff.
Henri, Adrian ('Tonight at Noon') 34
Herbert, George 133
Hill, Geoffrey 107, 121
Hill, Wayne F 77–8
historical aproach to teaching Shakespeare
    18
Hitchcock, Alfred 57
Hobby, Elaine 7
Holiday, Billie 56
Holinshed, Ralph (source for many
    Shakespeare plots) 18, 92
Holub, Miroslav 2
Hood, Thomas ('I remember, I remember')
    2–3, 128–9
Horace 103 footnote
Hourd, Marjorie, teaching *Macbeth* 92–3
Hughes, Geoffrey, author of *Swearing: A
    Social History of Foul Language, Oaths
    and Profanity in English* 6, 15, 78
Hughes, Ted 11, 20, 91, 104, 117, 128,
    132–4

iambic pentameter, the 27–9, 37, 59, 75,
    113, 126, 129
improper in Shakespeare, and children
    15ff.

James-Moore, Jonathan 12
Johnson, Samuel, views of Shakespeare 10

Kincaid, Eric 18
Kingsley, Ben (in film of *Twelfth Night*)
    131, 141
Kott, Jan 17

Lamb, Charles and Mary 18–19
Lamb, G F 20, 134
Larkin, Philip 29
Lawrence, D H, teaching 'Full Fathom
    Five' with an inspector present 4, 66
lesson plans 143ff.

Literacy and Numeracy National Project
    126ff.
literacy strategy, the 136ff.
luck, writers' 62, 66, 145

McCoughrean, G, stories from
    Shakespeare 17–18
McEvoy, Sean 6
Magical Realism and *A Midsummer Night's
    Dream* 39
management and managerialism 136ff.,
    143
Marquez, Martin 12
Martial 103 footnote
metre, formal 101
Meyer, Gerda 2
Meyer, Priscilla 2
Millais, John Everett (painter of *Ophelia*)
    133
Miller, Arthur 114–15
Morgan, Edwin 2

Nabokov, Vladimir 2, 109
names 42
national curriculum 18, 89, 106
Neill, A S, and Shakespeare and
    Summerhill 9
Nunn, Trevor (maker of the film *Twelfth
    Night*) 131

objectives 107
obscenity, children and Shakespeare 6,
    15–17, 56, 80
obscurity in children's writing 81
OFSTED 4, 136
Olivier, Laurence, directing the film of
    Hamlet 133
Opie, Iona and Peter 96
Orwell, George 10
Ottchen, C J 77–8
oxymorons in *Romeo and Juliet* and
    Macbeth 37, 108–11

painting, children's, inspired by *Hamlet* 22
paradox 37, 98, 108ff.
Partridge, Eric, and Shakespeare's bawdy 6,
    15–17, 91
Patten, Brian 34
Paul, St 138ff.
Pearce, Philippa 39

Pearse House (courses for young writers) 33, 43, 52, 70, 78
Peel, Marie 18
Pennington, Michael 12
philosophy and children 70
physical education, warm-up, compared to writing warm-up 62
Picasso, Pablo 39, 127
Plath, Sylvia 2
play, with a significant double meaning 1, 22, 46, 102, 124, 143–4
plenary sessions in lessons 62
plots, Shakespeare's – but not his 7, 18–19, 21
Polanski, Roman, *Macbeth* film 4
Police, The ('Every breath you take') 49–50
politics, present-day, and Shakespeare 3ff.
Pound, Ezra ('make it new') 144
Pryce, Jonathan 12

Raine, Craig 2
Reid, Gina 101
rhyme 49, 51
rhythm 101, 127, 131
Ricks, Christopher 121
riddles 63–4
Roeves, Emily 16 footnote, 103 footnote
Rosen, Harold 36
Rosenfeld, Mordecai, on rote learning 129–130
rote learning 124ff.

Scannell, Vernon 11
Sedgwick, Dawn 70
sentimentalisation of Shakespeare 11, 19, 77, 94
Serraillier, Ian 18
Seymour-Smith, Martin 15–16
Shaw, G B, on Shakespeare 10
Shepherd, Simon 7
silence, and children's writing 94, 144, 148
similes 40–2
Simmonds, Jean, as Ophelia 133

Sonnets, Shakespeare's 20, 109, 112, 127, 129
special needs, children with, and Shakespeare 43
'standing orders' for getting children writing 94, 144–8
Stillman, Francis 28
Stowe, Alison 131–2
Strauss, Richard 129
Stride, John 12
Styles, Morag 6
Summerhill School, and Shakespeare 9
swearing 6, 15, 78

tape recorders, composing with 148
Terfel, Bryn 121
testing, children and education 3–4, 96–7, 124, 136, 140
Theroux, Paul 4
Thomas, Edward 61
Thompson, Denys 102, 124, 130
Titanic (film) and children 65–7, 72
touchstone, memorised poems as 128–9

Vendler, Helen 20
violence in Shakespeare and children 7, 11, 90, 108

Wannamaker, Sam, and his Globe theatre 17
Weil, Simone 140
Wheale, Nigel 6–7
Whitehouse, Mary 15
Wilson, John Dover 19
witches in *Macbeth* and qualms about them 90–91
Woodhead, Chris 6
word processors, composing with 148
Wordsworth, William 5, 26–7
writing by teachers 20, 97

Yeats, W B 13, 127
Yiddish, a production of *Macbeth* described 114